Practical social work

Published in conjunction with
the British Association of Social
Series Editor: Jo Campling

Social work is at an important stage in its development. The profession is facing fresh challenges to work flexibly in fast-changing social and organisational environments. New requirements for training are also demanding a more critical and reflective, as well as a more highly skilled, approach to practice.

The British Association of Social Workers has always been conscious of its role in setting guidelines for practice and in seeking to raise professional standards. The concept of the *Practical Social Work* series was conceived to fulfil a genuine professional need for a carefully planned, coherent series of texts that would stimulate and inform debate, thereby contributing to the development of practitioners' skills and professionalism.

Newly relaunched, the series continues to address the needs of all those who are looking to deepen and refresh their understanding and skills. It is designed for students and busy professionals alike. Each book marries practice issues and challenges with the latest theory and research in a compact and applied format. The authors represent a wide variety of experience, both as educators and practitioners. Taken together, the books set a standard in their clarity, relevance and rigour.

A list of new and best-selling titles in this series follows overleaf. A comprehensive list of titles available in the series, and further details about individual books, can be found online at:
www.palgrave.com/socialworkpolicy/basw/

Series standing order ISBN 0–333–80313–2

You can receive future titles in this series as they are published by placing a standing order. Please contact your bookseller or, in the case of difficulty, contact us at the address below with your name and address, the title of the series and the ISBN quoted above.

Customer Services Department, Macmillan Distribution Ltd, Houndmills, Basingstoke, Hampshire RG21 6XS, England

Practical social work series

michael preston-shoot

effective groupwork

second edition

MT

First edition 1987
Second edition 2007

Published by
PALGRAVE MACMILLAN
Houdmills, Basingstoke, Hampshire RG21 6XS and
175 Fifth Avenue, New York, N.Y. 10010
Companies and representatives throughout the world

PALGRAVE MACMILLAN is the global academic imprint of the Palgrave Macmillan division of St. Martin's Press, LLC and of Palgrave Macmillan Ltd. Macmillan® is a registered trademark in the United States, United Kingdom and other countries. Palgrave is a registered trademark in the European Union and other countries.

ISBN-13: 978–1–4039–0552–9
ISBN-10: 1–4039–0552–5

This book is printed on paper suitable for recycling and made from fully managed and sustained forest sources.

A catalogue record for this book is available from the British Library.

A catalog record for this book is available from the Library of Congress.

10   9   8   7   6   5   4   3   2   1
16   15   14   13   12   11   10   09   08   07

Printed in China

6/7/07

Contents

Acknowledgements

I would like to thank Jo Campling and Catherine Gray (Palgrave) for inviting me to complete a second edition and for being so patient when the task took much longer than I had originally planned.

I would like to thank all the students and experts by experience with whom I have worked and from whom I have learned so much. I also have greatly appreciated the support from my colleagues in the Department of Applied Social Studies, University of Bedfordshire.

I am grateful to the editors and publishers of the journal *Groupwork* for permission to use my 1992 and 2004 articles as the basis for Chapters 2 and 9 in this book.

Two summer vacations were spent in Espinas (France), with the villagers encouraging me not to be diverted from the task of writing, and checking, sometimes daily, how many words I had typed. I have valued their interest in my work as well as the opportunity to become part of their group.

Finally, I owe so much to Suzy Braye. I dedicate this second edition to her as a small token of my profound appreciation of everything she is.

Luton   Michael Preston-Shoot

Introduction: locating groupwork

Since the first edition was published (September 1987) social work has changed considerably. In terms of practice values, anti-oppressive perspectives have become central. Consequently, groupwork may have been defined too tightly (Brown, 1996): monocultural, ethnocentric, prescriptive and unresponsive to diversity in its delineation. Service user involvement has become far more significant, expressed through such principles as empowerment, partnership, citizenship and social inclusion. Relationships between practitioners and service users have changed, in espoused theory if not also in theory in use. Service users are seen as experts on defining their own situation and on pursuing change. This change is captured by Fisher (2002) who describes how social workers are specialising less in what causes individual difficulties and social problems and more in individual and social processes that involve people in (re)discovering and applying how to help themselves. This repositioning now extends into social work education, in the United Kingdom at least, since service users must be involved in the recruitment and selection of students, in teaching and assessment, and in the management of social work degree programmes (DH, 2002).

The practice context has witnessed and continues to undergo structural change, requiring knowledge of and skills in working in, across and between groups. Adult services are experiencing closer alignment, if not integration, of health and social care, stimulated by the Health Act 1999 and the Health and Social Care Act 2001. New organisational forms are emerging, with social (care) workers and professionals allied to health employed by care trusts.

In youth justice, multidisciplinary youth offending teams have been created by the Crime and Disorder Act 1998. In planning and in service delivery youth justice social workers must work alongside the police, probation officers, teachers, youth workers and health professionals. In children's services, similar emphasis is given to needs assessment and planning, requiring consultation and agreement between a wide range of agencies which, at an operational level, are then central to assessment and intervention for family support and/or child protection. The Children Act 2004 has strengthened duties on agencies concerned with young people's well-being to work together. They must cooperate to improve young people's outcomes in respect of health, safety, achievement, behaviour, and employment and training. The Act also allows resources to be pooled in order to promote cooperation. In requiring the appointment of a Director of Children's Services and in establishing a joint inspection and review framework, the Act also integrates education and social services.

Across these services and between these sectors there remains an urgent need to understand group and organisational processes – the dynamics between and use of power within and among groups. Inquiries into mental health, community care and childcare tragedies regularly highlight distorted, disrupted and/or damaged relationships among agency and professional groups (Laming, 2003; Reder et al., 1993; Reder and Duncan, 1999; Sheppard, 1996). Whistleblowers (Hunt, 1998) and inquiries (Waterhouse, 2000) have also revealed disturbing and abusive practices. Themes of dehumanisation, demoralisation, insecurity and powerlessness emerge from research as experiences of social (care) work staff and 'clients' (Preston-Shoot, 2003a).

In this context Ward (2002) refers to problems derived from a failure to apply knowledge and understanding of group process, and to use groupwork skills in agency and task management. He suggests that an understanding of groups might illuminate the mosaic of agencies that now straddle practitioners' and managers' experiences of work. The Protection of Children Act 1999 and the Care Standards Act 2000 are attempts, through registration and inspection duties, and through closer monitoring of staff recruitment, to ensure that providers of care are meeting the highest standards. While welcome, increased regulation alone may prove insufficient to ensure lawful and ethical practice (Preston-Shoot, 2001). There is certainly a need, then, to reappraise groupwork's potential as one space for policy and practice change when seeking an effective response to the critical challenges that managers and practitioners face.

This is truer still because social policy has become preoccupied with public safety at the expense of individuals' due process rights;

with control, authoritarianism and individual responsibility; and with disillusionment with penal and welfare agencies. Policy-makers consistently invoke images of risk posed by groups as diverse as young offenders, asylum seekers and people with severe mental distress. The practice landscape has also been reconfigured by the modernisation agenda (DH, 1998), with its emphasis on standards, accountability and quality. The high profile now given to effectiveness and to outcomes has generated the introduction of performance targets and national service frameworks. There has been a renewed emphasis too on the relationship between research and practice, as evidenced by the publication of knowledge reviews by the Social Care Institute for Excellence. In practice, education for professional practice and policy-making, effective ways are being sought to ensure use of research (Walter *et al.*, 2004). However, the concept of evidence, or what counts as knowledge, is contested because of what approaches to research and which research users and producers it prioritises, and what assumptions it makes about decision-making, planning and work.

Social work has undergone something akin to a rollercoaster ride. Sometimes derided for its value base, criticised for its skill base and challenged on its knowledge base, alongside some other pro-fessional groups in the last decades of the twentieth century it was mistrusted. It was caught up in and reshaped by government criti-cisms (James, 1994; Clarke *et al.*, 1994) of welfare for being pater-nalistic and creating dependency, and of professionals and their agencies for being self-serving, inefficient, unresponsive and monopolistic. More recently its concern with inequality, injustice, oppression and poverty has found some support in government endorsement of the international definition of social work (IASSW, 2001), which identifies social work with concerns for social change and human rights. A more positive 'spin' from government on social work refers to its importance. This has been accompanied by a determination to raise its profile and standing. Registration of social (care) workers, publication of codes of conduct (GSCC, 2002) and the launch of the three-year social work degree are evi-dence of a shift in perception. Nonetheless, state social (care) work is low on confidence and hesitant about its role in influencing social policy. Disillusionment remains (Audit Commission, 2002; Preston-Shoot, 2003a). Since it remains a truism that staff cannot empower service users if they do not feel empowered themselves, Brown's observation (1996) is pertinent: managers (and policy-makers) need good group facilitation skills, currently undervalued in a managerialistic culture, if changes in social work education and practice are to be managed successfully.

There have been questions about whether groupwork can survive in a work environment where procedural practice and managerialism dominate (Preston-Shoot, 2004). Yet groupwork is a method of choice with a wide range of client groups and issues (Heap, 1992; Pollio, 2002). In part this is because even the most troubled individuals can make use of it (Ward, 1995). In part it is because groupwork can engage people at different levels (Mullender, 1996) – intrapersonal, interpersonal, socio-psychological, socio-structural. In part it is because it address themes central to professional activity – powerlessness and hopelessness, guilt and shame, denial and resistance, acceptance and support (Shulman, 1988).

Arguably, groupwork literature and practice have struggled to keep pace with these changes. Books still tend to present a basic framework for planning, facilitating/leading and managing groups, although different perspectives, models or approaches are being voiced. Such divergence may crystallise around conceptualisation of group stages, attitudes towards group size, or involvement of users in the definition of need and design of service response. There is now a dedicated United Kingdom journal, *Groupwork*, the contents of which reflect to some degree the changes that have taken place or are occurring in the social work world. However, its appearance was once erratic and, like most social work literature, its impact on practice remains aspirational rather than proven, even though it offers examples of practice informing theory-building and theories for practice. Nonetheless, here too is evidence that, whether or not there ever once was, there is now no one groupwork theory or practice.

So, the initial task is to locate groupwork within the changing policy and organisational context for practice.

1 | Practice and potential

Introduction

This chapter will map groupwork practice in social work and social care. It will survey current practice and identify groupwork's potential as an intervention, a strategy to effect change. This will include drawing upon research that provides evidence of groupwork's effectiveness. The contribution of groupwork to the modernisation agenda (DH, 1998) will be discussed.

Mapping groupwork

Groupwork continues to occupy a variable position within social work, sometimes central, sometimes peripheral, increasingly invisible. Within probation this has allowed Caddick (1991) to report that groupwork is well-established, while Senior (1991) has concluded that it has struggled to be located in the mainstream, partly because of managerial ambivalence about innovative practice.

For some practitioners groupwork represents a method of working effectively with a wide range of groups, a different approach to the challenges that confront them, and an antidote to casework's limitations in meeting people's needs. Its attractiveness lies in the value position it can enhance, a means of expressing and enhancing people's common humanity, and a commitment to social justice. It formalises a conviction that people can be understood and helped only when considered alongside the networks and systems in which they live, and that human services should connect and use the identification of people's strengths to address not just individual needs but also social divisions and structural inequalities.

For other practitioners, however, groupwork remains a peripheral or extracurricular activity on the fringe of social (care) work, something difficult to incorporate into overstretched workloads or to integrate within the traditional approach to the organisation of social services. Indeed, while it is difficult to establish the exact extent of groupwork practice (Doel and Sawdon, 2001), concern has been long-standing about the declining prospects for undertaking groupwork in many agencies (Smith, 1988) and about the disappearance of groupwork skills (Doel and Sawdon, 1999a). Ward (2002) asks where groupwork has gone.

One reason for this variable position, and perhaps decline, is that more often than not groupwork is another demanding responsibility placed on top of an already substantial workload and undertaken without supervision or amidst managerial scepticism. Jones (2001) has argued indeed that social workers are unsupported, overburdened and depleted physically and emotionally. Habermann (1993), offering a similar international perspective, implicates poor working conditions and large caseloads. It requires, therefore, a high degree of commitment and enthusiasm for any practitioner to contemplate groupwork and to establish a continuity of experience that allows the development of their skills and knowledge as groupworkers.

Both Ward (2002) and Doel and Sawdon (1999a) implicate managerialism and the growth of procedural rather than professional practice. Indeed, policy for practice emphasises conformity to regulations, management of precisely framed and time-limited tasks and achievement of prescribed performance targets and outcomes over relationships and informed use of methods and skills as part of a process. In their research, Marsh and Triseliotis (1996) found that students and newly qualified practitioners emphasised skilled process and interpersonal work in contrast to the pragmatic expectations of employers. Hardly surprising then that supervision should be criticised for being unconcerned with personal and professional needs or with theory (Preston-Shoot and Agass, 1990). Moreover, the impact of this practice change has been insidious. Barnes (2002), bemoaning alleged deficits in social workers' skills and methods and reporting that carers expect a mix of specialist and generic approaches, found social work preoccupied with risk assessment, objective-setting and monitoring rather than methods of intervention. The evidence, then, points to a demethoding and deskilling of social work, which allows other disciplines and professions to expand their use of groups (Kurland and Salmon, 1993).

Thus, groupwork is out of kilter in a disciplinary climate of preset objectives and audited outcomes (Ward, 2002) because, as Papell (1999) and Manor (1989) have also observed, groups have a life of their own and may pose problems for agencies. Group-workers cannot completely control them or determine the direction of change that develops. Indeed, they would perhaps wish to support people's right to express different meanings in the spirit of open inquiry, to validate the excitement of difference (Lordan, 1996). A commitment to anti-oppressive practice would certainly entail encouragement of recognition of different elements within a particular situation. However, by contrast, Brown (1996) notes that many workers are creating and facilitating groups when they are being oppressed rather than empowered by their employing agencies. This suggests other factors at play, and that groupwork retains a potential powerful enough to attract practitioners operating otherwise in a climate where social work has lost considerable control of the ends to which it is put and the means of achieving them.

Certainly unhelpful is the brief acknowledgement given to group-work in qualifying courses and in-service training, which historically has meant practitioners feeling ill-equipped for the task (Davies, 1984). That policy surrounding social work education has all too often been ahistorical is demonstrated by the recurring theme of limited academic preparation as one reason for group-work's decline (Reid, 1988). Marsh and Triseliotis (1996) found that groupwork was omitted from social work training for some students and that, while nearly three-quarters of their respondents spent some or a lot of time working with or in groups, only two-thirds felt adequately or well prepared for this task. Groupwork featured well behind family work, counselling and task-centred methods in the frequency of approaches and theoretical perspectives influencing practice.

Similarly, Mathias-Williams and Thomas (2002) found that final-year social work students gave groupwork far less prominence than conducting assessments, providing support and counselling, complying with legislation or providing information, when identifying their most important tasks. Barnes (2002) reports that students want their training to provide a greater understanding of methods of intervention. Arguing that social workers lack basic skills and that training must pay greater attention to their development, she reports that service users expect practitioners to have skills in and an ability to offer therapy work. Education and training, she suggests, should provide a deeper grounding in social work theory, methods of intervention and their practice application. However, when arguing for students needing to learn about and to practise skills, Barnes refers to cases. This betrays another constraint on groupwork's development, namely social work's casework inheritance – its focus on individual work and remedial or therapeutic problem-solving – which has meant that the development of groupwork skills and programmes has been a low priority for social workers (Heap, 1992). Some commentators (Papell, 1992; Habermann, 1993; Kurland and Salmon, 1993) implicate a continuing preoccupation with the individual and with intra-psychic rather than interpersonal issues. Brown (1996) sees primacy having been given to the individual rather than the collective, to the market rather than to justice. Perhaps reflecting its loss of confidence in attempting macro change, social work has retreated to privatising personal issues.

Nor does this appear to be a uniquely United Kingdom phenomenon. Both Habermann (1993) and Kurland and Salmon (1993) provide an international comparative perspective. Here too social groupwork is omitted from practice and from curricula, or is deemphasised, meaning that students never achieve learning beyond an introduction to the method. The outcome is a vicious circle: the less training practitioners receive, the less groupwork is practised, the less training is then identified as being required. Alternatively, the less training is provided, the more students and practitioners are likely to feel not yet competent and the less likely then groupwork is to be envisaged as an intervention.

Another obstacle lies in the interaction between workers and their employing agencies. Practitioners may feel that to practise professionally requires clarity and specificity concerning the aims of the proposed group and the formulation of a proposal according to the assessment of the workers. However, to obtain acceptance of the proposal to lead a group and to enlist the cooperation of colleagues, practitioners may feel constrained to devise a group that is acceptable to their agency and to refrain from being too specific. Indeed, ambivalent agency commitment features in the literature. For example, Mistry (1989) clearly describes the difficulties faced by workers in acquiring funding and in establishing groupwork as a credible different approach to familiar challenges. Lumley and Marchant (1989) noted the isolation of many groupworkers.

A further obstacle may lie in a deep personal ambivalence about groups. Groups are central to everyone's lived experience but that experience may be mixed. If, as already implied, practitioners are concerned about their need for support and their lack of confidence, and anxious about what they perceive to be their limited skills and competence, they may also be ambivalent, even fearful about groups. Common fears include concern about a group's potential for destructiveness, about losing control or encountering unmanageable situations.

---

envisaging groupwork

Identify your feelings about groups and groupwork, namely:

1. What positive experiences have you had as a group member?
2. What negative experiences have you had as a group member?
3. What positive experiences have you had as a group leader or facilitator?
4. What negative experiences have you had as a group leader or facilitator?
5. What is the best and worst thing that could happen to you in a group?
6. What do you find easy in groups and what do you find particularly challenging?
7. What images of groups and groupwork have these experiences left you with?
8. To what degree, and why, have these experiences made it more or less likely that you will join groups or work with groups?

What is experienced, perhaps, is a series of push–pull factors. What drives people towards groups, such as the search for intimacy and connection, may also evoke anxiety. What keeps people away, such as a fear of rejection or a desire for autonomy and self-determination, may also evoke envy of the collective support apparently enjoyed by others. Pictures can graphically illustrate what might concern potential groupworkers: one individual speaking while other group members sleep; a groupworker acting as a go-between between two hostile subgroups; group members acting out 'difficult' behaviours while a groupworker looks lost; the power of the group that makes it difficult for an individual to raise an item or to voice a different opinion.

Actual personal experiences in groups of competitiveness, conflict and (ab)use of power create representational models that are then transferred into new situations which are seen as if similar or identical to the original encounters. Sharing personal experiences of groups, and being open to unlearning and new learning in training and supervision, is a necessary preliminary.

Realising groupwork's potential

If one challenge resides in personal ambivalence about groups and groupwork, another is located in professional recognition of the coexistence of opposites. Groupwork can be a source of empowerment but also a site of social inequality to people's detriment (McLeod, 2003). This tension is captured vividly by the group sequences in the film *One Flew Over the Cuckoo's Nest*. People can find empowerment and liberation through group membership. They can, however, experience being seen as difficult and destructive.

---

putting into practice: mapping groupwork

Survey your present work experience and the available literature, to identify:

1. The advantages that groupwork offers.
2. The disadvantages that groupwork might involve.
3. Ways of maximising the advantages and minimising the disadvantages.

Breton (1991) points to the powerful dynamic and benefit of mutual aid, and groupwork's ability to engage marginalised populations. Empowerment can be derived from awakening and/or affirming people's capacity to help themselves and others, and from realising that socio-economic and political forces have shaped their difficulties. Shulman (1988) refers to the potential that can be derived from:

● Strength in numbers, giving service users power over behaviour, the helping process and the environment.
● The healing power of being in the same situation.

● Using group process to reach into difficult areas or deeper themes.

Kurland and Salmon (1993) refer to groupwork's unique potential to help members learn and benefit from diversity, difference and commonality, to overcome the impact of stereotypes and to experience group process as a powerful dynamic for change. These advantages are akin to Yalom's (1995) curative factors. Groupwork offers possibilities of cathartic release and interpersonal learning, of the installation of hope and creation of universality from the realisation of having problems and identities in common. Group cohesion and altruism may be derived from identity and support. Thus, using both the above exercises with students commonly elicits such positives as experiencing support, strength in numbers, learning and sharing. Groups can be liberating and empowering, not least because they can link the personal with the political.

However, negatives or disadvantages also commonly emerge. Groups are seen as vulnerable to subgroups and to domination and oppression by more powerful individuals. They can threaten individual identity, involve loss of autonomy and prove destructive. Groups may fail to develop or may lose a shared focus, or they may be locations for conformity and powerlessness that group pressure can engender. While a possible site for support, for developing people's resources and for learning from feedback and modelling, they can equally reinforce stigma and labelling.

These personal expressions are echoed in the literature, which reports anxiety and lack of confidence, fears and fantasies, linked to a perceived loss of power and control and to encountering powerful emotional dynamics (Reid, 1988; Habermann, 1993; Ward, 1993). These images may make it difficult to trust that group process and dynamics will produce positive benefits, and may make workers reluctant to abrogate their centrality as *the* helping person in the group. Kurland and Salmon (1993), moreover, refer to the possibility that group process can be used by those with power to enhance conformity. One particular aspect of this phenomenon is *groupthink* (Janis, 1972). Beneath apparent unanimity reside pressure to conform and intolerance of difference. These phenomena are reflected in routinised practice, an absence of criticism or fresh ideas, and a lack of questioning of goals or reflection on possible alternatives.

Thus, leaders, facilitators and members hold groupwork's potential on scales. As Ward (2002) comments: groupwork can prove a source of different perspectives, support, power, information exchange, hope, belonging, role models and feedback. It can provide opportunities to learn and test skills, to help and be helped. It can break down isolation and be a place to experience power. Groups can empower, for instance when rooted in values of anti-oppressive practice which link private and public spheres and self-determined action. However, groupwork can be characterised by one-to-one treatment with onlookers or by a focus on individuals rather than on oppressive social conditions. Groups can compound disadvantage and discrimination if provision is not conducive to cultural needs. Brown (1996) adds that the increasing use of off-the-shelf groupwork packages can mean that members are fitted into preset parameters rather than a group shaped by interaction between people in a manner responsive to their needs. Such highly task-oriented groups often give minimum attention to group process and dynamics. They may provide a sense of security for groupworkers but need to be used flexibly and creatively if the benefits of working with people in a group are to be maximised.

Commonality, as a feature of groups, can also work both ways. Hill (2001) observes that members may experience relief when they find others with similar experiences, feelings and understanding. Groups can then prove a setting for hope, for learning and growth, for giving as well as receiving. However, Cohen and Mullender (2003) argue that the degree of commonality between people and their goals, and the extent to which people move towards progress, can be exaggerated. Pease (2003) goes even further, in another echo of groupthink, suggesting that commonality can lead to collusion.

How the scales tip will depend on groupworkers' values and knowledge, both in espoused theory and as theory-in-use. Nonetheless, groupwork's positive potential is now embedded in the national occupational standards for social work (TOPSS, 2002). Social workers must in future be prepared for and capable of working in groups to assess their circumstances and needs. They must be able to manage risk to groups and to plan, carry out, review and evaluate practice with groups. The standards further require them to:

● Help groups to make informed decisions.
● Sustain support networks.
● Advocate with groups.
● Assist people to become involved in settings where decisions are made.
● Help groups achieve planned outcomes for members and evaluate their work.
● Work with groups to promote individual growth, development and independence.
● Identify opportunities to form and support groups.

Values for such practice include demonstrating respect for and promoting the dignity and privacy of groups and communities; recognising and respecting diversity, expertise and experiences in groups and communities; and maintaining trust and confidence.

Nor can social (care) practitioners work as members of organisations without groupwork knowledge and skills for managing practice and working in teams. Thus, graduating social workers must not only be competent in helping people to gain, regain and/or maintain control of their own lives, and to understand and challenge inequality and discrimination, in which groupwork may be purposeful. They must also be knowledgeable about factors that facilitate effective interdisciplinary, interprofessional, inter-agency collaboration and partnership, and skilled in interacting within this context (QAA, 2000). This reinforces an earlier observation (Marchant, 1988) that learning to be a worker in a group is insufficient. Practitioners also need to be competent members of groups. This involves understanding processes operating in groups and skills in negotiating group and intergroup relationships in order to attain desired goals. The relevance, then, of groupwork should be obvious when considering that social work's key purpose (IASSW, 2001) is to promote social change, to solve problems in human relationships, and to enable empowerment and liberation of people to enhance their well-being. This is a transformative agenda of change in people's intrapersonal, interpersonal and social worlds. It is an agenda wherein groupwork knowledge, values and skills can be useful in all three major strands of social work (Payne, 1997):

● Reflexive–therapeutic – working for the well-being of individuals, groups and communities, by promoting growth

and self-fulfilment and enabling a fuller understanding of self and person-in-relationship with others.
- Socialist collective – using cooperation and mutual support to empower, to challenge oppression and to seek social justice.
- Individualist–reformist – using services to meet people's needs, to help them cope with their lives.

Perhaps, indeed, the possibilities for using groups are bounded only by the levels of awareness, imagination and groupwork skills possessed by staff, and by the support or advisory structures available to groupworkers (Mullender, 1990).

Groupwork's effectiveness

Evidence-based practice in pursuit of effective social work is now emphasised by government and professions alike. Humphreys *et al.* (2003) conceive of a triangle of research, practitioner and service user perspectives to inform practice. Journals and book chapters certainly provide substantial evidence of practitioner evaluations of groupwork's effectiveness. To varying degrees they also give voice to service user perspectives. However, some writers (Matzat, 1993; Hopmeyer and Werk, 1993, for example) note a lack of research and an urgent need for comparative studies to maximise the beneficial aspects of groupwork and to collect data for theory-building.

The nature of the research evidence is variable in support of claims of effectiveness. Sometimes the evidence appears anecdotal, even aspirational in tone, because evaluations summarise beneficial outcomes. More rare is where group episodes are identified to illustrate change, or where members articulate the difference a group has made for them. Rarer still is an evaluation of outcome by means of establishing a baseline with group members and then repeating the measures at intervals during and after the group's conclusion. Evaluative research on outcomes of groupwork practice and its conceptual base is scarce, making it difficult to advance groupwork as the intervention of choice or to distinguish between the merits of different options when planning and facilitating groups (Preston-Shoot, 2004). Locating the evidence for groupwork's relevance and value must be an imperative if it is to capture the space opened up by the social policy concern with effectiveness and quality, and to respond fully to the requirement (DH, 1998) that services should be evidence-based.

Claims are made for groupwork's powerful potential for individual and social change (Papell, 1992). On balance the evidence for individual change appears stronger than that for social change, perhaps because social (care) work is more likely to focus there. However, DeLois (2003) provides a groupwork account where members and facilitator owned inequalities, identified commonalities, focused on strengths and built a language of power and possibility, in so doing changing the nature of their interrelationships within and beyond the group. Mullender and Ward (1991) offer examples of self-directed groupwork making a difference in how agencies responded to group members. They and Ni Chorcora et al. (1994) demonstrate that groupworkers can develop partnerships with service users while working from state social work agencies, and can change existing power relations in the direction of promoting real dialogue and collaboration.

Nonetheless, if groupwork does make a difference to outcomes (Cohen and Mullender, 2003), then it is more often in the realm of intrapersonal and interpersonal change. Thus, bereavement groups (Hopmeyer and Werk, 1993) enable members to gain friends, voice feelings, share hopes and strengths, and find connection and support. They can find new ideas and understanding, and information on additional sources of help. The benefits are those of commonality, normalisation, solidarity, reciprocity and control.

Similarly, Hill (2001) provides evidence of the vital role of peer support in a group focusing on sexual abuse. It provided a safe and non-judgemental forum in which powerful emotions could be expressed and addressed, which often members had been unable individually to share with social workers. Once again, commonality with others, the hope and experience of moving on and the opportunity to talk through issues and difficulties, appear to change thinking and to be genuinely therapeutic and empowering.

Kohli (1993), working with deaf people, sees groupwork reducing the negative impact of attitudes and enabling increased insight into personal difficulties. The outcome is an opportunity to voice demands for social change and also an improvement in interpersonal functioning. Garrett (1995), working in a closed institution, found that groupwork could be humanising, could change behavioural norms and could reduce trauma. In a prison it could provide a community of enquiry based on listening and a deepening of respect, and provide learning that was experienced rather than taught.

Both self-help groups and worker-led or facilitated groups (Bodinham and Weinstein, 1991; Matzat, 1993; McKernan McKay *et al.*, 1996) can secure changes in self-perception and in how problems or issues are conceptualised. This is because group experience boosts self-esteem and growth, enabling people to feel stronger and more confident. It increases people's networks and contacts, reducing their isolation, and it increases their skills in resolving intra- and interpersonal conflicts. Group experience enables members to review their own situation – finding commonality, helping others, watching and listening to others (the influence of modelling) provide a different context through which to view one's own position. Group experience enables members to become agents of change for each other – providing support and challenge, (re)dis-covering resilience and strengths. It introduces people to different ideas and to the powerful potential of a collective. Finally, it can link private troubles with public policy and social issues.

The modernisation agenda

Social (care) work is being reconfigured by a whole raft of policy initiatives which stem from a White Paper (DH, 1998). Particular emphasis is being given to the provision of needs-led services that offer consistent quality and ensure that clients are safeguarded from poor practice. The promotion of people's independence is one clear aim; another is inclusion and involvement in service planning and development; a third is the promotion of choice in what services are selected. Targets for change include energising partnership working between organisations and service sectors, and with clients and their carers, and raising the status of social work. Evidence of the latter may be seen in the introduction of the three-year degree as the route to a licence to practise, registration, and acceptance of an expansive IASSW definition (2001) of social work's role and tasks.

Yet there is a contradiction. The policy context for practice is also characterised by exclusion, anxiety and control, especially concerning asylum seekers, people with mental distress and young offenders. Insecurity and fear, amplified by media and political comment, about the location and level of risk, mean that these groups are marginalised, perceived as dangerous, and/or demonised and dehumanised. With such groups social work is increasingly given a narrow role of risk assessment, surveillance and resource rationing. More generally, social work is increasingly being governed ideologically and technically (Lymbery, 2001) through the imposition of targets, regulations and standards, with best practice arguably distorted by the need to meet imposed indicators of effective performance (Preston-Shoot, 2001).

To this complex and contested landscape, where service users may also be sceptical of the policy language that offers choice and needs-led services, may be added the tension between practitioners and managers, at least in terms of what they prioritise. Research (Marsh and Triseliotis, 1996; Barnes, 2002) continues to highlight that practitioners emphasise process, interpersonal skills, knowledge from empirical research and methods of intervention. Managers emphasise procedural and instrumental skills, knowledge of the law and performance of agency procedures. Clients and carers, also, value process and relationships. However, mindfulness of the affective component of social work, including groupwork, fits ill with the new managerialism that values command and control, output measures and agency-defined tasks, even sometimes at the expense of ethical and/or lawful practice (Preston-Shoot, 2000).

The modernisation agenda could render groupwork's place in state social work agencies more fragile, or at least restrict its ability to embrace social change goals. Thus, agencies may only be prepared to support groups that address government imposed standards or service objectives. In relation to work with offenders, this is highly likely to mean groups that aim to prevent reoffending, that focus on an individual's needs and behaviours (Caddick, 1991). What is lost here is the dual perspective – individual and society, or individual-in-situation – which acknowledges and seeks to address the impact of the socio-economic context on people's needs and behaviour. A policy agenda of individual responsibility does not fit easily alongside social work's advocacy that understanding people's behaviour and needs must include attention to the impact of a lack of power and conditions of disadvantage. Groupworkers, to counter a narrowing of envisaged roles for social (care) workers and for groupwork, will have to seek those spaces (Preston-Shoot, 2003a) through which a plurality of focus can be maintained, the voices of service users heard, and the personal and political connected. One space may be found in partnership with service users and carers, building on their reported experiences. Another resides in the evidence-based practice agenda, enabling practitioners to restate how research should inform practice and to challenge how policy and services are configured and delivered. A third space is found, therefore, in the research literature, in empirical and conceptual accounts of practice, and in evaluation methodologies.

Nonetheless, the picture is not entirely bleak. Accountability is one clear theme within the modernisation agenda. Here groupwork can make an important contribution, particularly through a commitment to anti-oppressive practice. Thus, the codes of practice for social (care) workers (GSCC, 2002) refer, inter alia, to protecting the rights of service users and carers, to promoting their interests, and to supporting them to control their lives and make informed decisions. From the previous discussion of the positive outcomes of groupwork practice, it will be clear how, for example, groupworkers can facilitate self-directed groups to secure goals that members value. The power that comes from harnessing a group's resources might enable members, with or without the assistance of groupworkers, to advocate for their rights and interests. The requirement in the codes to maintain the trust and confidence of service users and carers may, for example, be achieved by the use of protocols concerning confidentiality and the use of positional or statutory authority, by shared recording, and by clear contractual agreements about values and roles.

Indeed, the Association for the Advancement of Social Work with Groups (AASWG, 1999) has produced a set of standards for groupwork practice. While it assumes a traditional groupwork model rather than also embracing self-directed or other models where groupworkers are facilitators rather than leaders, it is nonetheless a welcome statement because it identifies groupworker tasks at different group phases. It also sees the group as the primary source of change, using helping relationships, and considers mutual aid to be central to groupwork practice. The groupworker's role is to help members achieve the goals *they* have established for themselves. There is an emphasis on empowerment, on group goals emphasising both individual growth and social change, with the groupworker promoting individual and group autonomy. Groupworker–member relationships are to be characterised by egalitarianism and reciprocity.

In other respects, too, groupwork may have an important contribution to make to the modernisation agenda, as Table 1.1 illustrates.

Table 1.1 Connecting groupwork with modernisation

Key principles from Modernising Social Services (DH, 1998)	Examples of how groupwork may contribute to the realisation of principles
Services should promote people's independence and respect their dignity	Values, knowledge and skills that aim to realize groupwork's beneficial outcomes – promoting resilience, strengths, resources, capacity and power
Services should meet people's specific needs	Manage problem-solving, manage transitions and change processes
People should have a voice in services that are provided and how	Values of, and practice using, self-directed groupwork; theories explaining group and organisational behaviour, adaptation and change
Services should be underpinned by clear and acceptable standards that are enforceable	Standards for groupwork practice; methods of intervention, including knowledge of factors guiding choice and evaluation of them
Coordination between agencies and professional groupings	Knowledge and skills for forming learning organisations and new working partnerships and interprofessional teams. Understanding what promotes cooperation within and between teams, groups and organisations
Flexibility and responsiveness	User and carer involvement; promotion of self-directed and self-help groups. Developing relationships and partnerships that facilitate change. Attention to themes from group process and dynamics
Quality	Researching and evaluating outputs and outcomes
Role clarity	Standards for groupwork practice

Mapping need

The modernisation proposals (DH, 1998) are based on a ministerial conclusion that many social services departments were not identifying trends in need or demand, and were unable to adequately assess and prioritise need. Systems of support for children and families and for vulnerable people such as those fleeing domestic oppression, survivors of mental distress, homeless people, and adults requiring support to maintain life in the community (for example, older people and learning disabled people) were not needs-led. Additionally there were gaps in provision.

Other researchers have also found that most agencies did not understand the pattern of need and were struggling to quantify volume and type of services required. Government inspections have also concluded that local authorities continue to have significant gaps in information and that their track record on involving other agencies is poor (SSI, 1999). They struggle to survey and identify at-risk or vulnerable groups, or to systematically analyse unmet need.

Subsequently, planning and the assessment of need have become core features of the modernisation agenda – to secure better services, to obtain better outcomes for service users, to focus service development, and to facilitate community and individual capacity-building and social inclusion. Local authorities have been charged with profiling need and reviewing provision. They must identify groups for whom provision is missing or inadequate, prioritising the meeting of needs of groups at risk of harm or presenting the possibility of risk of harm.

However, assessment of needs is complicated by uncertainty about what should be measured and by the difficulty of knowing how to 'capture' it. Further challenges arise from the likelihood that actual and potential service users, carers, and health and welfare practitioners and managers will hold divergent perspectives. Various stakeholders' definitions of need will represent different but interacting ways of thinking about need and of determining approaches to outcomes (Godfrey and Callaghan, 2000). Nonetheless, identifying and responding to need have always been a core component for effective groupwork and there are various methodologies that can be employed to research needs in order to inform service development. These include:

● Community needs profiling (Green, 2000) – focusing on issues such as poverty, housing and unemployment, to provide information on micro and macro levels. Data collected may challenge established views of particular localities or groups.

They can inform practice by, for instance, highlighting where groupwork and other service developments can strengthen existing networks or create new provision.

● Social audit (Percy-Smith, 1992) – an approach to policy formation and evaluation, assessing the extent to which objectives have been achieved. It provides information, including measures of shortfall between need and resources. It can pinpoint formal and informal assets in communities, thereby contributing to assessing their actual and latent capacity to promote people's well-being (LASSL (2000)).

● Needs assessment (Percy-Smith, 1996) – provides data on the relationship of need to social problems and on outcomes, for example by comparing and contrasting the perspectives of service users, their carers and the professionals involved with them. It can generate data on the effectiveness of current means being employed to secure desired outcomes.

● Service take-up data (Hare *et al.*, 2002) – identifying people known to agencies and considered vulnerable, at risk or in need. Combined with community profiling, it can highlight geographic areas where there are high levels of need and/or service take-up, and where more input appears indicated.

If these methodologies can be employed to identify the range and level of need, from which to devise targets and objectives, how can groupworkers map need? Green (2000) lists a number of methods, namely interviews, surveys, focus groups, observation and use of secondary data (statistics, census information, service take-up rates). A population profile, using primary research and secondary sources, may not be possible for most groupworkers because of questions of cost. Equally, for some service user groups at least, it may not be appropriate because the incidence of need is likely to be low and, therefore, a random sample is likely to produce a lot of redundant information. Response rates may prove problematic and there is a limit to the volume of data that can be collected by questionnaires. However, groupworkers can research professional judgements about people who may be 'in need' and can triangulate these data with those obtained from interviews with actual service users and from a picture of referrals to different agencies.

Focus groups can prove a more efficient way of collecting information than individual interviews (Raynes *et al.*, 2001).

Considerable information can be collected in a short time frame while enabling respondents to be part of a support system when discussing issues that could prove sensitive or difficult (Walton, 1996). They facilitate exploration of experiences and access views, for example of services and gaps in provision, and how these might be remedied, from marginalised populations whose voices can be silenced, obscured or misrepresented in surveys. They enable experts by experience to feel more comfortable in responding than might be the case in individual interviews, where the power imbalance between worker and respondent is starker, and allow them to offer creative insights into attitudes, feelings and experience. Such rich qualitative data can enhance policy and practice development.

---

putting into practice: auditing needs

What questions might you want to research about the needs of a client group with which you work? To answer these questions, what groups exist with which you might interact to gain additional perspectives? What focus groups might you create for the purpose of answering your research questions?

Focus groups are a structured and disciplined method of promoting voice and engaging people in sharing expertise and experience (Swift, 1996) and in compiling and analysing data (Ward, 1996). However, focus groups do require active facilitation to overcome any problems with dominant individuals and to keep participants focused on specific topics and questions (Home, 1996).

Need, however, is a slippery concept since it involves distinguishing between normative need (defined by experts), felt and expressed need (an individual's personal assessment) and comparative need (defined against a standard) (Bradshaw, 1972). The more sources from which information can be gathered, the more needs can be triangulated, that is, mapped against these different distinctions (Percy-Smith, 1992). This will help to ensure that definitions of need do not lapse into a service-led or professional-led approach, and an expert-led model of service development (Everitt *et al.*,

1992) where how questions to be asked are formulated and how issues are constructed are quite likely to reflect dominant power structures (Fisher, 2002). Incorporating a service user perspective locates clients and communities as 'knowers', thereby aligning research with emancipatory and anti-oppressive practice, concerned with the redistribution of power.

So, how do groupworkers know that a problem or need exists? How do they know that it is *this* problem or need that should be prioritised? How does their research lend empirical support to identified need (Kolbo *et al.*, 1997/98), and what does the research reveal about sources of support or resistance to their proposed approach? In other words, how do they know that the need for their proposed group is real (Doel and Sawdon, 2001)? It is to this and other practice questions that the focus now turns.

Practising groupwork

The next eight chapters will take the reader through planning, leading or facilitating, and managing groups. They will contain evidence from research and from groupworkers' own accounts to cement the links between theory and practice.

The term 'groupwork' complicates the situation since it is an all-encompassing description of activities which vary from group therapy and social groupwork to social action, self help and consciousness-raising. Some groups are problem-centred, others are not. The intention may be to alleviate social isolation, to prepare people for new experiences, to resolve or prevent problems, or to provide some form of learning opportunity. There are a variety of theoretical frameworks and leadership styles so that it can be difficult to identify which knowledge base is the most appropriate. Some approaches emphasise individual-centred aims and focus on the needs and reactions of individuals. Others stress the importance of group-centred aims or social change goals. These groups may concentrate on attempting to change social attitudes towards group members or to tap members' capabilities, which are overshadowed in other social work methods that emphasise individual needs. The result is that groupwork can appear a daunting enterprise.

Numerous practice-related questions confront practitioners wishing to explore groupwork:

- Which clients might benefit from which types of groups?
- How might the group be presented to potential members so as to engage them?
- How should members be selected and the length of the group determined?
- What guidelines are available on forming a group?
- What should be a group's focus and how might groupwork become an economical use of resources?
- How can groupworkers include all the group's members and keep to the format of the group?
- How might groupworkers enable a group to become self-supporting and hand back the leadership role to members?
- How might groups mirror social divisions, for example those of 'race' and gender, and how might groupworkers practise anti-oppressively?

Immediately, however, how these questions are formulated betrays assumptions, for example that groups are formed by social (care) workers who select members. Other questions, perhaps, hint at roles for both members and groupworkers in planning and facilitating the group's focus. The presumption here is that there is no one groupwork theory or practice. Rather, the challenge for groupworkers is to find their own theory of practice, and to (re)discover their own groupwork voice. Models, such as those offered in this section, describe what *might* happen, not what *should* happen (Schiller, 2003). In that sense, complexity has replaced simplicity in groupwork theory-building, which should not be interpreted as necessarily either unidirectional or neatly segmented from inspiration to conclusion. There is no one size fits all (Williams, 2003).

Indeed, Mullender and Ward (1989) deliberately set out to challenge familiar assumptions through their advocacy of self-directed groupwork. Here the emphasis is on facilitation rather than leadership by groupworkers. How the group is conducted – issues of frequency, location, focus and timing of meetings – is negotiated. Members are not selected but are more generally part of already existing groups, or are approached.

Theory is essential for informed practice, while practice should evaluate and inform theory, a circular process of making sense of experience. Every practitioner carries around theories and belief systems which determine what is looked for and the sense made of experiences. These beliefs are shaped by gender, 'race', culture, socialisation and training. If not acknowledged and critically appraised, they can box in a practitioner. In place of curiosity, a dialogue with oneself and with others, there is a bias that can result in the dismissal of possibilities.

---

putting into practice: personal reflection

> ➤ What do you believe about groups?
> ➤ Who or what has helped shape these beliefs?
> ➤ To which groups have you previously belonged? What has this membership 'taught' you about groups? How do you carry this experience into those groups of which you are a part today?
> ➤ What knowledge, values and understanding characterise your approach to groupwork practice?
> ➤ What experiences have contributed to your particular formulation of groupwork practice?

Theory, then, should be less a forced march and more a map of walkways, offering different standpoints from which to understand complex terrain. This book, therefore, aims to set out some basic questions and to attempt some answers; it also aims to enhance the reader's awareness of the issues and sense of the feasibility of groupwork. It offers a practice guide for social (care) workers either involved or interested in groupwork. With its emphasis on promoting skills in the preparation for and leadership or facilitation of groups, on what promotes effective planning and evaluation of groupwork, the book aims to equip groupworkers with a structure for practice and to bring some sense to a complex process. Each chapter that follows will outline key practice issues and offer some guidelines. There will generally be no differentiation between social (care) work settings, types of groups, or 'client' groups since the skills and tasks involved are substantially the same and the framework applicable whatever the setting or type of group envisaged. Rather, the stages and processes of groupwork will be described.

2 | Practising groupwork values

Introduction

Groupwork is a process of enquiry, discovery and action in which all participants are prepared to engage. It is a shared endeavour towards resolving problems or circumstances felt by participants to be both real and urgent. However, how is this process to be conducted?

Social work is always value-laden since it is bound into political, economic, organisational and knowledge structures which influence how practitioners formulate, plan and lead or facilitate groups. Values shape what is seen, the sense made of this, and what knowledge is privileged and used. For example, if one aim of a group is adjustment, this implies acceptance of conventional values rather than attempts to change norms. If social (care) workers ignore or are confused about values, the goals they formulate may not be relevant to what members bring to groups. They may be unable to respond to what members say affects them and their received ideas and assumptions will remain unchallenged. Indeed, there has been evidence of ineffective, unethical and even abusive practice. Sometimes this originates in workers and service users holding divergent views about targets for change or the means to achieve them. Sometimes professional intervention is not research-informed and produces depressing outcomes. Sometimes it has involved the use of manipulative or coercive techniques, or undermined individuals and their networks, or locked people into dominant assumptions about, for example, gender and family (Preston-Shoot, 1992).

Moreover, social work requires its practitioners and managers to negotiate familiar practice dilemmas and the questions they raise:

- Care versus control – what values and principles should we operate?
- Welfare versus justice – what criteria should determine the intervention?

● Needs versus resources – are services needs-led or provider-led?
● Humanitarianism versus economics – are considerations of cost or effectiveness to predominate?
● Agency versus professionalism – to whom are practitioners accountable?

Groupwork has not escaped these dilemmas. The distinctive features of one model include the conjunction of care and control, of individual-centred aims arising from user need with agency function and its statutory context (Brown et al., 1982). Such groups are leader-centred, particularly in relation to aims, membership and structure. However, a user-centred paradigm challenges many basic assumptions about groupwork planning and practice (Mullender and Ward, 1991). It emphasises user control of group design, focus and aims, and social change goals involving the confrontation of oppression and entrenched mechanisms of power.

Brown (1996) categorically states that a core condition is that groups are anti-oppressive in content, purpose, methods and relationships. Why? Without an explicit anti-oppressive value base, groupworkers are likely to replicate power and status relationships (Lordan, 1996; Brown, 1997) and provide an unequal and prejudiced service (Lumley and Marchant, 1989). Indeed, Senior (1991) is critical of groupwork's lack of attention to inequalities, such as those based in age, 'race', gender, disability, sexuality, poverty and class, and failure to respond to the real needs of disadvantaged groups. He urges groupworkers to redefine people's problems as shared political experiences. This leads groupworkers away from an approach that individualises and pathologises people's difficulties towards one which recognises the impact of structures and socio-economic as well as interpersonal relationships on how those difficulties are expressed, experienced and responded to. It leads groupworkers away from a focus on people's inadequacies towards building on the recognition of their strengths, skills and capacities. Working with offenders, for example, acknowledges the link between offending and socio-economic status (Mistry, 1989). It works not just with individual needs and behaviours but also with offenders' needs, experiences and behaviours as people in and affected by a social and cultural context (Caddick, 1991). Change can be initiated at individual, group and organisational levels.

However, in agency contexts where statutory duties dominate and define practice, how can groupworkers adopt and retain an approach centred on anti-oppressive principles and goals? This chapter explores a values frame for anti-oppressive groupwork practice, recognising that it has been all too easy historically for professionals to underestimate people's capacity for resilience, involvement, creativity and change.

Towards an anti-oppressive values frame

Mullender and Ward (1991) perhaps offer the clearest, most explicit articulation of values in a groupwork context. Their value base for self-directed groupwork comprises the rejection of negative labels, such as assumptions of individual inadequacy, and the belief that people have skills, values and ability. They assert people's right to be heard, to be in control of their lives and to choose the interventions in which they will engage. They recognise that people gathered together can be powerful and that the exercise of such power is necessary given that the problems they face are complex, frequently involving issues of oppression. To practise anti-oppressively requires that oppression be challenged. Groupworkers provide facilitation rather than leadership, acknowledging that they are not the only source of skills and knowledge.

Similar explicit principles emanate from a strengths and empowerment model (Nosko and Breton, 1997/98). This model comprises four elements:

1. Respect – practice that challenges internalised oppression, identifies what people have in common, gives them voice and affirms their competence.
2. Self-determination – practice that trusts members, stimulates mutual aid, mobilises strengths and affirms people's choices. Groupworkers act as facilitators who may challenge members but who do not impose ideas or solutions.
3. Individualisation – practice that eschews preconceptions about ways forward, rejects labels and enables sharing of strengths.
4. Maximising use of supports in the community – practice that sees the community as a resource, that seeks to create partnerships and to modify or create structures to meet people's needs.

For Brown (1996) anti-oppressive groupwork practice focuses on the whole person, redressing structural and internalised oppression, and emphasising empowerment, mutuality and the release of people's expressive qualities. Lee (1991) focuses on connecting the personal with the political, groupwork seeking to develop efficacy in personal, interpersonal and political power. Groupwork is aiming to change structurally oppressive environments and individually internalised negative valuations, and thence to improve transactions between people and their environments. The intended outcomes are enhanced individual and group identity, resources and competence, coupled with restructured situations and improved environments.

In essence, this values-based approach recognises people's resilience and capacity for growth and change. It emphasises their competence, or their capacity to become competent, and envisages groupwork as a space where these capabilities can be identified, developed and utilised, and where members can experience how their actions can create change and increase their sense of control. This approach also recognises that environments and systems impact on people, making it difficult if not impossible for their strengths and competencies to operate or develop. These environments typically undervalue, dismiss or ignore people's narratives, which may therefore affect their engagement and result in social exclusion. For example, when seeking to involve experts by experience in working groups, organisations should recognise how engagement is affected by prior experience, the (lack of) available resources, agency (in)flexibility about payment, and assumptions about how such groups work in terms of modes of participation, location, duration and time of meeting.

Application of values to practice

Historically the terms 'anti-discriminatory practice' and 'anti-oppressive practice' have been used interchangeably. However, the former is reformist. It seeks to change unfairness or inequity in the way services are delivered but within officially sanctioned rules. Consequently it may not fundamentally challenge the structures that maintain inequality. Relationships between practitioners and service users are characterised by partnership and consultation about needs and preferences. Anti-oppressive practice is more far-reaching, engaging practitioners and service users with the wider societal context, seeking a fundamental realignment of power and relationships, beginning with an acknowledgement of structural inequalities and exploitative legal, social and economic relationships, and their impact on individuals and groups. Focus is given to how power has been used to define people's interests. The emphasis is on empowerment: mutual education, the suspension of assumptions about services and the creative exercise of power to maximise people's control over choices (Preston-Shoot, 1992).

This distinction between anti-discriminatory and anti-oppressive practice may be encapsulated in the differentiation between traditional and more radical values (Table 2.1).

The belief that group members have the ability to be self-directing and a responsibility for the direction of their learning and change efforts encompasses a belief that they have a capacity to diagnose their own needs and decide from a range of alternatives. Group members should have the maximum possible involvement in all stages of the groupwork process. The groupworker's task is to ensure that members are aware of their rights, of what groups can achieve and the range of alternatives, and are enabled to define their wants and needs in the group. That is, they should participate in formulating the group's aims and groupworkers should be interested in their views since they are involved in a process of learning, change and development to which members can contribute. The extent of this participation may vary. However, especially with young children, learning disabled people and offenders,

Table 2.1 Comparing values

Traditional values	Radical values
Respect for persons	Citizenship
Focus on needs	Focus on rights
Paternalism and protection	Participation
Equality of opportunity	Equality
Anti-discriminatory practice	Anti-oppressive practice
Partnership	Service user control

Source: Braye and Preston-Shoot (1995).

groupworkers should not underestimate members' abilities or undervalue their rights and should seek to enable them to voice concerns and take action on them. For example, in groupwork with offenders, it is appropriate to focus not only on changing members' attitudes towards offending but also on enabling them to take up those concerns that they see as contributing to their situation.

The commitment to people's narratives, empowerment and individualisation means that members' experiences are significant and that a group should begin with and respect these. Members will have critical powers, skills, knowledge and abilities to offer each other, resources on which the group can draw for support, learning and collective action. If members' experiences are devalued or ignored, this creates an atmosphere in which the assumption flourishes that they are passive recipients. It denies a part of their identity. A group should encourage and enable members to identify the capacities they are bringing to it with which they can help each other. This commitment assumes that members' statements are not necessarily symptoms of illness or deviance but those of ordinary people facing particular circumstances.

There are difficulties in implementing this commitment. It is not always possible to know when members' opinions and perspectives have been understood. Members may be over-eager to agree with groupworkers or may voice what they believe is expected of them or will avoid awkwardness. How groupworkers present themselves to members, help received in past encounters, and people's knowledge of services and groups may also shape how they present their experiences and relate to the current group. They may have experienced feelings of powerlessness, isolation, exclusion and hopelessness, which arise by virtue of being clients and the more disadvantaged members of society. This may make them reluctant to engage or keen to articulate their stories at every opportunity, each potentially making it difficult to move forward. Therefore, they may need encouragement, validation and support to translate their narratives into focused action. Groupworkers need to articulate clearly that participation can alter these features significantly, that members can address the power and control which others have over their lives by questioning others' attitudes to them, by challenging norms and by being involved in decision-making.

The commitment to facilitation and respect means that groupworkers are not experts who alone possess an understanding of the needs and dynamics of a group and its members but are resources in a process of enquiry and development. They may put forward their knowledge, opinions and experience and they may be responsible for the group's programme. However, their expertise lies in their capacity to engage the group in exchanging and developing knowledge and skills to meet its tasks, to help members understand their problems or concerns, and identify methods of tackling these collectively or personally. Group members may be unwilling to relinquish a view of the groupworkers as experts and leaders or unable to accept that the leaders do not have solutions to prevent, manage or eradicate problems.

Closely connected with this value stance is the concept of authority. Groupworkers should examine this concept from the members' perspective. Authority can arise from:

1. Position – conveyed by the role groupworkers hold, for example in statutory orders.
2. Representation of others – delegated organisational authority where an organisation has ultimate power.
3. Wisdom – authority derived from experience, knowledge and skills.
4. Influence or example – authority given by members to groupworkers because they see them as an appropriate model.

Groupworkers can hold authority in one or more of these categories at the same time. However, how they see their authority may differ from how agencies or members see it. Open discussion of authority may render how power is or is not used more intelligible and accountable. Anti-oppressive groupwork practice emphasises the third and fourth sources of authority, which groupworkers commonly see as enabling them to practise groupwork effectively. Thus, Schiller (2003) talks of practice that is non-hierarchical and that includes a willingness to share oneself, thereby connecting power and authority with relationship and empathy. Groves and Schondel (1997/98) emphasise practitioners as facilitators and catalysts, with experience and skills of relevance to the work envisaged, rather than as experts. However, members may see the groupworkers' authority as emanating from the first two sources. Indeed, groupworkers may find themselves having to exercise these types of authority. Some focus may be necessary on differences in perceptions of the groupworkers' authority and pertinent questions here include:

- Where would I reflect the standards and authority of the agency?
- Where do I consider it appropriate to mirror society and where to question it?
- To whom do I feel that I owe accountability in the final analysis – to my employer, to a code of ethics and conduct, or to experts by experience?
- Which values imposed by organisations would I agree with even where they are not accepted by clients? Which would I dispute?

---

putting into practice: working through issues of power and authority

---

➤ Identify situations where you have accepted or rejected another person's authority? What influenced your decision? What helped or interfered with you acting on that decision?

➤ When in your work do you feel powerful? Where does this power come from? When in your work do you feel powerless, and why? What does it feel like to be powerful or powerless?

➤ How does your exercise of power and authority empower or disempower service users? What power and authority do users have? How easily may they exercise it in relation to you and your agency?

➤ Identify a group in which you are or anticipate working. What power and authority do you need to work there effectively? What power might you transfer to users? How might you enable users to identify and use their power and authority? What do you feel about giving up power and control? What effect would this have on your work?

Clearly, different participants will have access to different types of power and authority. A prerequisite for empowerment and partnership is, therefore, an acknowledgement of power imbalance arising from material and social disadvantage, professional language and mystique, and discrimination. From this it follows that practice must seek to use and enhance the authority held by experts by experience, while recognising that professional power and authority remain, legally mandated, and may have to be exercised on occasion without user consent or cooperation. However, since this involves the transfer of power from workers to users, some focus on feelings about control is essential. These feelings may reflect anxiety about relinquishing control, the destructive potential of groups or trusting and working with group processes. Otherwise the worker's response may be to emphasise control and professional expertise, to adopt a directive approach and, thereby, to close down expression of opinions and feelings and limit learning opportunities.

Values informing group process

For Lee (1991) group facilitators will be empowering and acting anti-oppressively when they collaborate, share power, involve members in the change process, and build on people's problem definitions, strengths and collectivity. Group process here then is characterised by working alongside members. Group facilitators use their resources of networks, training, advocacy, knowledge and skills to enable members to share and acquire information, knowledge, skills and resources. Gutierrez (1990) similarly envisages an empowering process as accepting and exploring people's problem definitions, identifying and building on members' existing strengths, and engaging in a power analysis of the situation or issue that has brought them together. It may also involve mobilising resources and advocacy, or teaching specific skills.

The practice dilemmas inherent in social work and groupwork, and the organisational cultures in which practitioners are located, can make it difficult for groupworkers to identify their resources and to practise on the basis of clearly articulated values. For practitioners to work in partnership and to be experienced as empowering, they must themselves feel empowered.

---

putting into practice: professional role

What would colleagues and experts by experience say are encouraging and discouraging patterns in the way you work? What would you identify as your resources – values, knowledge, skills and experience? What have you learned that helps you to negotiate practice dilemmas and to work in partnership? What have you learned that obstructs it?

Equally, given the impact of racism, sexism and other forms of oppression on personal values and the professional task, practitioners must engage in reflection here too if they are to enable service users to challenge the way power is exercised. Senior (1991) identifies the threat to women-only groups from sexism in the probation service. Cohen (2003) stresses the importance of identifying, acknowledging and validating diversity as a prelude to empowerment and collective action. She warns, however, against the adoption of unhelpful simplicity – women, for example, are not (just) a homogeneous group, dichotomised from men.

---

putting into practice: working through oppression and discrimination

Ask yourself the following questions with respect to class, 'race', gender, sexuality and (dis)ability:

➤ How would I describe my identity?
➤ How, if at all, is that different from how I would have described it before?
➤ When was I first aware of my identity?
➤ When was I first aware of people whose identity was different from mine?
➤ What messages did I receive about my identity and that of other people?
➤ What effect has this had on my personal relationships and professional practice?
➤ When have I discriminated against people with an identity that differs from mine? What do I think makes me do this?
➤ When working with people whose identity is different, what is the impact of who I am and of my behaviour on them? What is the impact for me of who they are? How do differences affect our working together? What might be important for the people we are working with in relation to these differences?

Essential to effective practice also is a clear understanding of how partnership can be defined and is being applied in particular situations. For instance, are facilitators reaching out beyond groups known to them to those who are hidden, hard to reach and/or hard to find (Braye and Preston-Shoot, 2005)?

---

putting into practice: defining partnership

> What do you understand by partnership? How far and in what ways does your groupwork practice reflect working in partnership? How would group members know that you are working, or wanting to work, in partnership with them?
> Think about a group with which you are working or proposing to work. With whom are you in partnership? How far towards working in partnership have you gone? What level of partnership are you working at and what does this include? What more could you do to work in partnership in this group and what facilitates or hinders this?

Partnership may be seen as a continuum (Arnstein, 1969; Pugh and De'Ath, 1989), from involvement and consultation in decision-making processes within predetermined limits controlled by service providers to collaboration in defining issues and options, and beyond to user control. Partnership does not necessarily mean that participants have equal power. It does imply recognition and open discussion of how power is distributed and used, including addressing the different levels of participatory power with which members begin. It means clarity regarding the extent to which group members are involved in or control decisions regarding duration, focus, size and membership. It requires facilitators to maximise levels of involvement and to validate different types of participation (Braye and Preston-Shoot, 2005).

Values informing group content

Lee (1991, 1999) envisages a pre-empowerment stage. This focuses on raising consciousness of inequalities and of the dynamics and impact of oppression. She envisages here a journey from frustration with systems to impacting directly on them, from self-blame to speaking bitterness, and from hopelessness and isolation to connection with others and mutual aid.

The idea that poverty and economic insecurity, lack of rights and entitlements, and the physical and/or psychological impact of the use of power equate to powerlessness will be familiar. However, continued negative experiences when interacting with one's environment and/or negative self-evaluation by those oppressed and/or the environment blocking attempts to take effective action (Ni Chorcora *et al.*, 1994) may result in the internalisation of oppression. Lack of validation from others can prompt a lack of positive identity, which can result in a loss of skills and agency as the individual expects to be revictimised, in what becomes a vicious downward spiral. Group members may be unaware of their internalisation of oppression (Groves and Schondel, 1997/98).

Internalised negative valuations inhibit change just as much as direct power blocks applied by others (Lee, 1991). Passive acceptance is characterised by three features: personal blame (it is my fault), globality (it is like this everywhere) and stability (things will never change). This is why a first step for groupworkers may be to attempt to reduce the powerlessness generated by negative valuations, whether based on private experiences or membership of a stigmatised group. Consciousness-raising and identification with others may enable people to reappraise their position. Movement here may be characterised as increasing acceptance of universality (anyone would feel), specificity (it is just this situation) and transience (things can change).

There is, of course, another side to this coin. It may also be necessary to address internalised domination (Pease, 2003). Anti-oppressive practice challenges how those in dominant groups draw on, even if they do not always benefit from, such domination. Consciousness-raising and the linking of the personal with the social and political are key tasks here too.

This pre-empowerment stage is preparatory to an empowerment stage when the group can work on issues effectively.

putting into practice: defining empowerment

> What might experts by experience find empowering or disempowering about your groupwork planning and practice?
> Consider groups of which you have been a member. What have you found empowering and disempowering about these experiences?

Some empowering interventions are common to all groupwork. These include:

- Scene-setting and creating a safe space for the group's work.
- Normalising members' experiences, such as when joining a group.
- Listening and demonstrating a concern to understand.
- Providing information and counteracting professional mystique.
- Identifying and developing members' skills and strengths.
- Exploring what may be blocking the group's work (unrealistic goals, conflictual relationships, other systems, inadequate resources, different motivations).
- Allowing time for good communication to build and concentrating on how participants can use outside the group what they have gained from and within it (Braye and Preston-Shoot, 2005).
- Becoming less central as the group develops (Heap, 1966).

Mullender and Ward (1989) refer to helping groups discuss the nature of problems and possible solutions, and reflect on the process of the group and its work. These interventions can counter powerlessness and promote personal and interpersonal change. However, the concept of empowerment is limited if seen only as a form of enabling by professionals (Adams, 1990) as opposed to naming injustices, exploring power relationships and acting on the experiences of socially excluded groups (Cohen and Mullender, 2003). For Lee (1991, 1999) and Gutierrez (1990), empowerment involves developing individual and group consciousness in order to envisage and reach for personal liberation and social justice.

Mandates for anti-oppressive practice

To what extent is this values-informed groupwork practice possible? The inclusion of an expansive definition in the requirements for the United Kingdom social work degree (IASSW, 2001; DH, 2002) requires a focus on individual change *and* social justice, on problem-solving in human relationships *and* empowerment and liberation of people. The codes of conduct (GSCC, 2002) require that social (care) workers safeguard and promote the interests of service users and carers, and advocate for their wishes and views. Experts

by experience may, of course, mistrust this professional commitment, which represents a potential barrier, the reasons for which
must be acknowledged and challenged through the difference that
such a groupwork encounter can make.

Experts by experience want social workers to understand what
people's lives are really like and not to make assumptions about
needs (Barnes, 2002). They require practitioners to have cultural
awareness and understanding to ensure that the needs of diverse
minority groups are met. They want critical fixers (Braye and
Preston-Shoot *et al.*, 2005), namely, practitioners who are competent in effecting change but also prepared to engage in developing
a shared understanding of why such change is necessary.

The law may, perhaps surprisingly, provide a mandate for anti-
oppressive practice. Space may be found not just within legislation
designed to counteract discrimination on grounds of 'race', gender,
disability, age, sexuality, language and religion, but also in measures within childcare and community care law. Partnership is clearly
endorsed in policy guidance underpinning the Children Act 1989
(DH, 1999), while the Children Act 2004, through the creation of
a Children's Commissioner for England, provides an example of the
law attempting to change the status of a social group. The availability of direct payments within community care law represents a
measure aiming to develop the independence, choice and autonomy
of service user groups. The usual mindset is to envision the law as
a barrier to anti-oppressive practice but such provisions as the
Human Rights Act 1998 may enable practitioners to perceive the
legal rules more positively.

Conclusion

Groupworkers can strive to develop a values-informed practice,
enhanced by knowledge and skilfully implemented in relation to
themselves, their employing agency and group members (Preston-
Shoot, 1992). This represents one standard by which practice can
subsequently be judged.

Values

Practitioner–self

● An ability to confront personal values and assumptions, and
  the impact of these on personal and professional development.

- An ability to examine personal strengths and gaps.
- An ability to take and use feedback.
- A commitment to anti-oppressive behaviour.

Practitioner–agency

- An ability to appraise critically agency roles, tasks and functions, and the relationship between these and wider socio-political values.
- A willingness to identify and challenge oppressive and discriminatory policies and practices.

Practitioner–group members

- A commitment to principles of user autonomy and participation; to developing the strengths and resources of group members; to protecting and empowering those at risk of, or experiencing, abuse and exploitation; to the value and dignity of individuals.
- Identifying and challenging oppressive behaviour.
- Promoting practice that actively challenges racism, sexism, disablism, ageism, heterosexism, and issues related to class and poverty.

Knowledge
Practitioner–self

- A critical understanding of power and authority, of sources of inequality and oppression, and of social constructions of childhood, gender, ethnicity, age, sexuality and disability.
- Ability to use supervision and learning for personal and professional development.
- Understanding competing theoretical perspectives on group development, leadership and process.
- Understanding competing theoretical models of inequality and its impact (consensus and conflict models of authority and social relationships; medical and social models of disability and health).

Practitioner–agency

● A critical understanding of the impact on agencies of political, social, legal, economic and racial factors, and of the reproduction through agencies of structural inequalities.
● Knowledge of agency decision-making and policy-making structures, and how to gain entry into these.
● Knowledge of agency policy and practice in relation to inequalities, equal opportunities and groupwork.

Practitioner–group members

● A critical understanding and application of models of group leadership/facilitation, process and development.
● Understanding the impact on individuals and groups of social and cultural constructions of inequality and oppression, of social policies and legislation.
● Knowledge of how power is exercised through images of gender, race, competence and status.

Skills

Practitioner–self

● Addressing the manifestation in groups of structural inequalities and the use of power and authority in groupwork planning and practice.
● Connecting the personal and political, groupwork practice and its context.
● Using awareness of the impact of self on others.
● Understanding and managing the complexities and tensions inherent in anti-oppressive practice.
● Applying the values of user empowerment and partnership, and managing the resulting practice dilemmas.
● Managing accountability to the group and the agency.

Practitioner–agency

● Using power and authority creatively to address imbalances of power between users and agency.
● Managing the dilemmas between different roles and sources of authority, and between personal and agency values.

- Representing the tasks, roles and functions of the agency to users, and enabling users' views to be heard within the agency.
- Avoiding authoritarian or defensive practice.
- Assessing agency effectiveness in promoting anti-oppressive practice, challenging attitudes appropriately, challenging assumptions within how problems are defined and solutions framed.
- Promoting groupwork, partnership and empowerment in the agency; involving practitioner and manager colleagues in planning and using groupwork.

Practitioner–group members

- Identifying power issues in group process and how these are influenced by race and gender.
- Addressing conflict and difficult issues.
- Engaging with expressed feelings.
- Facilitating the group's work in respect of coming together, building trust, discovering resources and experiences, sustaining commitment, defining problems and taking action.
- Integrating theory and knowledge of anti-oppressive practice, empowerment and partnership into planning and the group's work.
- Connecting the personal experiences of powerlessness with wider themes; identifying issues of inequality.
- Promoting non-exploitative relationships through information exchange, mutual education, working in partnership, support, addressing oppressive behaviour, moving between the group's centre and edge depending on the process and task stage of the group.
- Evaluating with members the outcome of the group.

The chapters that follow aim to provide groupworkers with additional tools with which to use their knowledge and skills for a values-informed practice.

3 | Types and purposes of groups

Introduction

This chapter will review the different types of groups which practitioners may establish or join, and the different purposes for which groups may be used. By discussing the various types of groups, their purposes and applications, practitioners may be encouraged to be clear about what type of group they envisage. This requires that they identify their main and secondary purposes for a group and the values and theoretical frameworks which they are seeking to apply.

What is a group?

Groups vary greatly in character and type. They can be long- or short-term, ongoing or time-limited, with a closed or open membership. They may be led by one person or more, or be self-directed where, if present at all, the groupworker has a facilitating role. They may rely on open or topic-orientated discussion or on exercises and games. Groups may aim to foster support or social interaction, or to provide opportunities for members to develop their potential abilities, to use untapped personal resources or to resolve particular problems. They may focus on common problems experienced by members outside the group or on issues and difficulties experienced by members within the group. Alternatively, they may be orientated towards social action, focusing their efforts on problems or circumstances which may or may not be experienced by members but which have implications beyond the group itself. Groups can be formed, with members drawn together by social workers, where membership may be compulsory or arise from an offer and acceptance of this offer. Other groups arise spontaneously, members coming together through circumstances or common concerns, such as housing or community facilities, rather than through the interventions of an outsider. Some groups are small, allow face-to-face contact, and encourage the formation of relationships that foster mutual identification and influence. Other groups are large and less intimate, where mutual identification occurs not through meeting but through some interest, common bond or characteristic. Increasingly in a technological age, members may meet in 'new' ways, via telephone conferencing, video link or use of email and web. The key ingredient, though, is interaction around a common interest, need, objective, problem or activity.

Groups are also naturally occurring phenomena within the life cycle of every individual. These groups include the family, school classes, peer groups, political parties and professional or staff groups. They may or may not be mixed in terms of gender, ethnicity and other social divisions. This variety in size, origins and purposes makes definition complex.

This book considers one variety of group with which social (care) workers are concerned. This is a group whose members choose to involve or agree to the intervention of a social worker and where the leaders have a professional duty and obligation to these members. It is a group where the leaders may or may not have been responsible for its formation but where their role is to help members work together and achieve the group's aims.

How may this group be defined further? First, it is a collection of people who spend some time together, who see themselves as members of a group and who are identified as members by outsiders. Brown (1996) refers to this core condition as mutuality/interaction. By definition, therefore, this includes groups formed by social workers and preexisting groups where members have come together and where the social worker chooses to intervene. Two examples of preexisting groups are a tenants' group formed by residents for the purpose of campaigning for improved housing conditions, and a group of learning disabled people formed for the purpose of moving into supported housing in the community. The definition requires members to have some physical proximity and implies recognition of the boundaries of the group.

Second, members may or may not expect to continue meeting, whether face to face or by means of technology, indefinitely. Some groups are time-limited, the duration fixed by the groupworkers and/or by members. The length of others may be determined by progress within the group towards a stated aim, for example action to improve the level of investment by a local authority in a particular geographic area. In ongoing groups circumstances such as age, interest, need or physical location will shape attendance. Here members rather than groupworkers take responsibility for the length of their membership of the group, perhaps exiting once they have acquired desired information, or found that their needs for support or problem resolution have been met.

Third, direct interactions and exchanges are possible between members who are interdependent. This implies that a group is not an alternative setting for one-to-one social work but a context where each member experiences several interpersonal relationships which, together with the members' contributions and the group's dynamics, may be used to help members reach their goals as individuals and for the group. Ward (2002) differentiates between work in groups and groupwork; Doel and Sawdon (1999b) between people in a group and people acting as a group. In the former, the group is a setting where the primary focus is not group dynamics or process. This may be a team, for instance, where the key relationship is between members and the team leader. Alternatively, it may be the location for work with individuals on particular problems or issues, with other members acting more as observers than participants (Reid, 1988), what Kurland and Salmon (1993) refer to as casework in a group setting.

Groupwork, however, actively uses group process and relationships between members. The group itself is the medium or instrument for help or change (Ward, 2002), members working together and using group resources, such as their commonality or diversity, support and interaction, to facilitate learning, to clarify perceptions, to confront barriers to communication and to develop strengths. Put another way, there is a dual focus (Kurland and Salmon, 1993), the exact calibration dependent on the group's purposes – work with and by individuals, together with how others respond to solutions or ways forward found by their colleagues, and analysis of group interaction, communication patterns and roles. This part of the definition implies, then, that the group's progress depends on the contribution of the total membership, on their capacity to act as a group towards the stated aims. Accordingly, not only do members need to work cooperatively but also they should understand and accept the purposes towards which they are working.

Fourth, the group is established for one or more purposes. The group may decide to work on a common goal, this shared purpose being their reason for meeting. Certainly, working on shared goals and mutually agreed tasks can prove enormously satisfying, motivating and enriching. It may promote a sense of identity or unity, which defines the group to others and legitimises its existence.

However, especially at the beginning of a group, members may not share a common goal. For example, in a group for young offenders, perhaps where membership is compulsory, members may hold different attitudes to and goals for the group which, in turn, may differ from the workers' purposes. The use of different types of contracts with members (Preston-Shoot, 1989) recognises that a common purpose, say in social or problem-solving groups, is not always necessary for members to feel valued for their contribution, to value other members or to experience a sense of belonging to the group. Indeed, a common purpose may be unattainable and it may be more productive to accept that working together contains elements of mutuality and of reciprocal exchange, agreeing to work on each other's needs and objectives.

If groups are formed where members and leaders disagree on their objectives in coming together, where the leaders or facilitators find themselves opposed to the group's objectives, or where members' purposes differ, three conditions are required for effective groupwork. First, leaders or facilitators must be clear that working with this group does not contravene their value base or ethical principles. Second, some agreement is necessary about short- or medium-term objectives if the group is to be established, a reasonable consensus among members concerning what the group is for and how to proceed, on the rights and duties of members and leaders, and on guidelines for behaviour in the group. Aims should be realistic and feasible, with differences respected and contained in the group. Third, it should feel possible to work with the differences and towards a greater consensus in the group. Otherwise, it may prove difficult for the group to achieve its potential (Whitaker, 2001). This working agreement, which reflects the purposes of the group, may fall into one of four categories (Preston-Shoot, 1989):

● Preliminary contract: an agreement to survey what is being offered without commitment and to clarify expectations.
● Primary contract: a mutual agreement based on a common definition of the goals.

● Interim agreement: a trial period either because aims are not agreed or to establish whether the services offered are appropriate to the needs defined.
● Reciprocal agreements: in which workers and members accept that their purposes are not identical but agree to cooperate in helping each other achieve their different goals.

Fifth, groups with which social workers interact may or may not be congruent with the function or views of their employing agency. Since the support of colleagues is a necessary condition for effective groupwork, practitioners may adopt an approach which they believe their colleagues and agency will accept, one that is compatible with agency function, resources and expectations (Brown *et al.*, 1982). This may account for the finding (Doel and Sawdon, 1999a) that the mainstream groupwork model in the United Kingdom remains a group comprising between six and ten members, meeting weekly for up to two hours over an eight- to twelve-week period, focusing on individual change or support, shaped by agency function. Alternatively, however, they can devise a project that they consider to be ethical and effective, and then attempt to persuade their colleagues and organisation to endorse the proposal. This may involve them in challenging practices that are reflective of institutional racism or sexism. It may involve them in campaigning to change the attitudes and traditional approaches of their own organisation (Mullender and Ward, 1991). Social workers may find that they are encouraged to develop innovative approaches with client groups who appear not to respond to one-to-one casework or who add significantly to their agency's workloads. Equally, they may encounter indifference, hostility or mistrust, shown in the absence of interest or the referral of unsuitable clients. It is prudent to explore ideas with colleagues, with the aim of arriving at a consensus about the place of groupwork and the members who might benefit. Through discussing with colleagues their views, reservations and concerns, groupworkers will be able to assess whether their project will be effective in their work environment and whether it will involve isolation from or rejection by colleagues.

Besides the support of colleagues, a group is more likely to succeed if the workers are interested in the group and if it originates in demand or unmet need rather than in a worker's wish to extend their professional development. Of course, there may be occasions when a groupwork project is devised for staff or student training, or to try a new approach to old, familiar problems. However, a group is more likely to take off when it is based on an assessment of being an effective way to meet a situation. Therefore, a preliminary to an effective group is research into client and worker opinions from which a statement or map can be made of the needs identified, the resources already available, and the gaps in service provision. Put another way, a group should be a response to clients rather than clients being created for a group initiative.

It will be apparent that these part-definitions apply to a wide variety of groups. Similarly, definitions of groupwork which refer to social functioning or helping members to cope more effectively with personal, social or environmental difficulties can embrace a wide variety of types of groups and more specific objectives. Consequently, to make sense of the term 'groupwork' and to facilitate clear thinking and practice, social (care) workers need to classify types of groups. From this classification they can determine the type of group they envisage or are interested in.

The categories that follow are not mutually exclusive since one type can contain elements of another. What will emerge too is the interplay between the main activity of the group, the style of the groupworkers and the purpose of the group. The purpose of the group dictates the nature of the group and, to some extent at least, the style of the leaders or facilitators. The nature of the group is dictated by the way that the members and/or leaders perceive the purpose of the group.

Types of groups

Papell and Rothman (1966) classified groups according to whether the aim was remedial, social or both: that is, whether the aim was individual growth and rehabilitation, prevention of social breakdown, or mutual aid. Hartford (1972) differentiated according to whether the focus was individual (support, change, rehabilitation), interpersonal, problem-solving and task achievement (committee work, for example), environmental, or system change (pressure groups, for instance).

Social groups

These groups are defined by their content: social or recreational activities. The purpose of these groups may be to overcome members' isolation, to provide a positive experience of relationships, or more simply to offer an opportunity for pleasure. The groupworkers may assume responsibility for the group's activities or seek to encourage members both to offer suggestions and to contribute their own resources and skills for the benefit of other members. Members may be encouraged to take responsibility for parts of the group in the belief that this, together with enabling them to develop their interests and skills, can increase their sense of fulfilment and self-worth. Examples are social clubs for survivors of mental distress or older people, day centres and youth clubs.

Group psychotherapy

These groups aim to effect symptom relief and basic personality change. The emphasis is on enabling members to achieve their individual therapeutic goals. A variety of problems can be tackled effectively in group psychotherapy. Common among these are self-concepts like low self-esteem, lack of purpose and direction, and lack of a felt clear identity. Members may bring symptoms of anxiety, depression, ineffective coping with stress, poor performance at work or dissatisfaction with relationships. They may complain of emotional difficulties like the inability to express feelings or poor control over emotions. They may locate their difficulties in interpersonal functioning, usually described as the inability to achieve intimacy, discomfort in group situations, or lack of trust.

Members need to be motivated, wanting to change and prepared to work for it through self-exploration. Their wish to join the group should be voluntary and not the result of external pressure. They need to believe that the group will suit them and to accept the rationale on which group psychotherapy is founded. Since these groups rely heavily on verbal communication, members should be able to use verbal skills. A final requirement is psychological-mindedness, an ability to accept an appropriate psychological explanation of interactions and relationships within the self and between the self and others.

These groups have a present orientation, a here-and-now focus on what actually happens in the group between members, between them and the leaders, and between them and the group. There is a future orientation too, a focus on the goals of individual members, the options they possess, how they might choose from these and translate the choice into action. A focus on events that occur outside the group is discouraged, as is excessive historical inquiry into the origins of members' behaviour, although there may well be some focus on how transference and defence mechanisms become manifest among group members. The rationale for this process is that members can be helped to see that they are not unique, that they can derive support from other members as a result of which their resistance and reliance on habitual ways of relating will decrease and they can be encouraged to take risks. A further rationale is that members' behaviour in the group will be a direct reflection of their behaviour in life generally. These groups aim to enable members to become aware of their characteristic behaviours, with change emanating from a recognition of the ways members relate in the group and from using the encouragement and rein-forcement of the group to try out new ways of relating both within and outside the group. In this process the leaders attempt to steer the group into a here-and-now focus and may direct their com-ments either to individuals, subgroups or the whole group. A fuller explanation of group psychotherapy may be found in Whitaker (2001).

Group counselling

These groups focus on resolving particular problems or modifying specific situations. Usually members share a common problem or face a similar transition or life crisis. Focus is maintained on this problem or issue, which is clearly identified, and little attention is paid to other problems unless the group agrees to expand the focus. The problems may be practical and material, for example negoti-ating one's way through organisations dealing with welfare bene-fits, or they may be emotional and interpersonal. Here examples would include groups focusing on depression, isolation, bereave-ment, children who are beyond the control of their parents or who have been sexually abused, or difficulties facing step-parents on joining a family. One task for the workers is to help members identify and retain focus. Another is to enable members to build links between themselves. The groupworkers seek to enable the group to clarify the problem, to share solutions adopted by individual members and to help members individually and as a group to take decisions and to develop behaviours that relate to the demands of the situation. In focusing on the problem or issue, and the feelings that members hold in relation to it, environmental factors should not be overlooked either as contributory factors to the problem or as targets for change.

Educational groups

In one form of educational group, the purpose is to offer information and to impart skills through direct instruction. For example, a benefits group might aim to inform members of their welfare rights and to instruct them on how they may obtain these rights. A practical skills group might aim to introduce members to easier ways of dealing with practical problems in the home when on a low income and to provide an environment where basic skills are acquired through practice.

In another form, the purpose is to orientate and prepare members for life stages, new experiences and challenges, the prospect of which may arouse fear, uncertainty or disorientation. These groups focus on a change in status or position and work through the feelings aroused by transitions: from primary to secondary school, from school into employment, from early adulthood into midlife, from work into retirement or unemployment. Groups for people awaiting discharge from psychiatric hospital into the community, for prospective foster and adoptive parents and for couples hoping to have a child through assisted reproduction may fall into this category. There may be some information-giving but the emphasis is usually on developing abilities and behaviours and identifying strengths and resilience which have been underused or not needed previously.

In leading such groups, it is important to consider how people learn. Effective learning is less likely to come from without, from knowledge transmitted in a teacher–student format. It is more likely to follow from members' willingness to engage in shared learning to resolve difficulties or challenges felt by them to be real. It is more likely to follow from facilitated discovery and a willingness to participate in a process of curiosity and inquiry. Members con-tribute their own experiences, offer their ideas and knowledge to a shared learning process, acquire support from the group, and through discussion or simulation exercises consider how to approach the situation they are facing.

Social treatment groups

This cluster of groups may be subdivided into four. First, groups aiming to maintain adaptive patterns of behaviour and functioning or to enhance social functioning that is apparent already. These groups have a reinforcement and supportive orientation. Second, groups aiming to modify patterns of behaviour and functioning which may be disabling the individual. These groups have a change orientation. The purpose may be to enable individual members to give up redundant behaviours, adaptations that they have contin-ued to repeat after they have lost their meaning or to apply outside the context in which they were serviceable. Alternatively, the purpose may be to encourage members to give up behaviours that are defined as deviant and unacceptable.

Third, problem-centred groups aiming to improve members' abilities to handle and resolve problems. The group is concerned with specific difficulties located either within or external to the indi-vidual members. The group process and the influence of group members are used to achieve this aim. Examples include social skills groups, youth offending groups and groups for sexually abused children. Fourth, compensatory groups, where the aim is not so much to effect change but, through activities, to provide members with life experiences on which they have missed out. The aim is to compensate for this deprivation. Activity groups for children are one example of this type of activity.

Discussion groups

In these groups the focus is on the general rather than the par-ticular, on topics of interest to members rather than on specific difficulties or problems. The groupworkers' task is to create an atmosphere of trust and support in the group so that members may voice and develop their interests and use the contributions of other members. For example, groups in residential care may be used to enable members to reminisce or to contemplate what might improve quality of life in that setting.

Self-help groups

These groups may have a variety of aims, from campaigning for attitude or social change to using the group's resources for support and individual problem resolution. They can, therefore, deal with a range of problems (Habermann, 1990), using different configurations – open or closed membership, focusing on a formalised programme or member interests and on individuals or an issue outside the group (Matzat, 1993). They comprise people who feel that they have a common problem or need, often inadequately covered by statutory services, and who join together to address it. Accordingly, authenticity, reciprocity, equality, mutuality and a common language tend to be core components of self-help groups (Habermann, 1990; Matzat, 1993).

The attitude of professionals towards self-help groups has been ambivalent, sometimes idealistic, sometimes sceptical. Hill (2001) suggests both that professionals often do not understand self-help groups and that their assistance is, therefore, not always meaningful, and that service users hold back for fear of further losses. Members may find the concept off-putting and have to overcome their fears, of being judged for example, even when other sources of support have been extinguished. Personal contact with peers or a professional facilitator (Schneewind, 1996), then, may facilitate entry into the group.

Groupworkers may form a group with the purpose of becoming less central in or less responsible for the group, to the point where the group continues to meet without them. However, such self-help groups may fail if sufficient agency support is not forthcoming and if groupworkers withdraw from facilitation too hastily.

Social action groups

Cohen (2003) suggests that these groups encompass personal, interpersonal and political dimensions. Accordingly, where these groups are focused on structural analysis and macro change, nonetheless, those engaged in them may experience positive personal and interpersonal changes as a result of their participation. Those people engaged in social action groups for the purposes of interpersonal change may find that social divisions shift as a result.

Many people, whether or not they are clients of social welfare agencies, are trapped in social and economic deprivation. Social action groups aim to utilise a group's resources for collective power as a vehicle for campaigning for social change and for the rights as well as the needs of group members. These groups are often formed around issues like housing standards, community facilities or welfare rights.

Self-directed groups

In the groups identified above, the aims are identified either by the groupworkers or by them in conjunction with the group's members. In self-directed groups (Mullender and Ward, 1991), members rather than groupworkers determine the direction and objectives of the group. These groups may be problem-centred, focusing on problems which members raise. They require, as do self-help groups, that members work together and find their own solutions, not just from within the resources of the group members but through attempting to influence and change people outside the group. Like social action groups, they may campaign on issues arising from members' concerns expressed once the group has formed. A key goal often is some aspect of external change together with the development of members' self-esteem and assertiveness. The group identifies the skills, knowledge and abilities within it and these are harnessed to enable members to work on the issues that the group has identified. Thus, in self-directed groups groupworkers have a facilitative rather than a leadership role, which comprises (McKernan McKay et al., 1996) enabling group members to take decisions and to increase their sense of competence, to find material and access resources, and to experience success and to evaluate their work. The role is collaborative – knowledge and experience are offered to but not imposed on the group.

Using group classifications

This classification illustrates that groupwork can address a variety of aims and purposes, and that group types are not mutually exclusive. Rather, a particular design can incorporate features of several types of groups. Therefore, an early task for practitioners who intend to lead or facilitate a group is to identify the type of group they wish to be involved in.

---

putting into practice: framing a group

➤ Is the group a collection of individuals being formed by groupworkers for a specific purpose, or rather a preexisting group whose existence is being extended to cover a new purpose, or a permanent group for which the groupworker's knowledge may prove useful?
➤ Is the main focus on internal personal change, on interpersonal change, or external social action?
➤ Is the group self-directed or one where, at least initially, the groupworkers are central to how it manages both its task and processes?

In selecting from this classification, groupworkers will be influenced by the goals they and group members have in mind, the style of work and leadership or facilitation which they favour, and the value base which underpins their social work practice. Determining the type of group will be shaped by the objectives and aims with which the groupworkers begin. It should also be influenced and modified through a dialogue with members when social workers offer their services to an existing group or interview prospective members referred to a group which they are hoping to form. Having achieved a degree of clarity on the type of group to be conducted and the aims for that group, questions of structure such as size, duration and open or closed membership can be resolved.

Aims, purposes and uses of groupwork

Groupwork does have its limitations. Generally, groups cannot provide exclusive attention to an individual member. As discussed earlier, groups should not become an alternative setting for one-to-one work with the addition of an audience. Whether a group has goals that are defined in terms of social action, individual-centred

or group-centred aims, members will be required to work cooperatively towards these ends and, consequently, to put aside on occasions their needs or issues for the work of the group or for other
members.

Nor can groups be expected to provide immediate benefits.
Placing a number of people together does not mean that they function immediately as a group rather than a collection of individuals.
If, for example, one aim is that members will discover that they
share experiences in common, such commonality may take several
meetings to emerge, if at all. If one aim is to encourage members
to verbalise their feelings associated with their difficulties or circumstances, an atmosphere of trust has to be fostered before they
are likely to feel that it is safe to do so. Whether or not members
ultimately feel that the group is beneficial or empowering depends
on their commitment and the groupworkers' skills in promoting the
functioning of the group. Their ability to mobilise the group's
resources, of support, inquiry and care, may also depend on their
ability to overcome any legacy of powerlessness and the impact of
negative events.

The economic motive is questionable too. Social workers may
believe that their service delivery will be improved by seeing several
people at once. However, this apparently economical approach
involves considerable time and emotional commitment which
should not be incorporated into overstretched workloads. As
Lebacq and Shah (1989) discovered, working with children who
had been sexually abused, groupwork complemented but did not
replace individual work. Similarly, Habermann (1990) believes that
self-help groups complement but do not replace state intervention.
Moreover, groups do not necessarily achieve the aims that influence
social (care) workers to form them nor reduce the demands that
members may make on social work agencies. Indeed, the reverse
may be the case. Accordingly, groupwork should be adopted when
social workers consider it to be the best method available for tackling a problem or achieving a particular goal rather than as a
numbers exercise alone.

Another motive which social workers may have for using groupwork is to reduce the powerlessness, isolation and stigma attached
to members as individuals and as clients. Certainly, members may
gain considerably from meeting with other members. It is not
uncommon to hear clients express relief at the realisation that they

are not alone in their particular situation, that they are acceptable and have skills, knowledge and abilities which are valued and useful. They may feel less threatened by social workers if they have other members for support. Further, a group may find it easier than individuals alone to challenge and alter the labels, perceptions and attitudes held by those outside the group. However, bringing together clients in a group may increase their sense of separation and difference from others, both within and outside the group. It may reinforce the labels attached to them and widen rather than narrow social divisions, at least until the group can engage in purposeful work designed to change this context. Thus, social workers need to consider carefully how members might feel or perform within and outside the group and whether the benefits that might accrue from membership outweigh the perceptions which members and others might construct by virtue of their membership. Belonging to a group, of itself, does not change descriptions applied to members by themselves or by others.

The prevailing social policy context, with its preoccupations with risk and dangerousness, has meant that groupwork has increasingly been used for purposes related to social control and conformity (Caddick, 1991; Doel and Sawdon, 2001; Ward, 2002) rather than personal and interpersonal development. Members have often, quite literally, been outcast and may themselves therefore be at risk, notwithstanding whatever risk of harm they might potentially carry for others. While social control has always been one component of the role and tasks of social workers and probation officers, it is the values underpinning social policy regarding (young) offenders, asylum seekers and people with particular forms of mental distress, for example, which groupworkers may find incompatible with their professional ethics.

So what are the uses to which groupwork can be put? What aims and purposes can groups work towards and achieve? In what ways can group process be a catalyst for change? It is likely that a group will have several aims drawn from across the categories described below.

One set of purposes may be described as preventive. The problem of isolation may be tackled by the formation of a group with the aim of reducing its effects. Members may feel less alone by meeting others with similar interests or circumstances. Achieving a sense of belonging and mutual identity can lead to change in social relationships and to members being able to receive help or tackle situations or problems using the support, knowledge, ideas and experience acquired in the group. This preventive function may be seen too in groups which aim to maintain or improve functioning, for example in social skills, parent and child, and youth offender groups, where a programme is designed to enable members to develop more adaptive and functional patterns of behaviour or interaction.

Another use for groupwork may be defined as the purpose of achieving external change, of encouraging social action in the community in the pursuit of social change goals. No social worker can be unaware that the systems of which individual clients are a part, and in which they live and function, exert a considerable, often negative influence. Nor can social workers be unfamiliar with the feelings of powerlessness and alienation which clients experience, particularly with the emergence of a literature that presents the often critical perspectives of clients and carers on the work of social services departments. Unemployment, poor housing, poverty, inadequate community resources and high eligibility thresholds in many welfare organisations all impinge on clients of social work agencies. If social workers neglect these features, they omit an important, influential part of the reality of their clients' lives and limit the extent and impact of their change efforts.

Groups that incorporate the purpose of social action aim to challenge received assumptions concerning the powerful and powerless. They redefine clients' needs as clients' rights and hope to achieve improvements in their environment and living conditions. Social action groups campaign on issues, establish provisions such as social clubs and playgroups, and interact with representatives of such agencies as the police and housing departments. Members often select targets of change themselves. If the attitudes or behaviour of the members change, this is seen as occurring through the emphasis on and achievement of social action as opposed to concentration on these attitudes or behaviours themselves. A specific aim within the overall purpose of social change goals is to improve communication and interaction between members and between them and the systems outside the group. A further subsidiary aim is to achieve a change in the way other systems perceive group members. If this is achieved, a change may follow in how the members perceive themselves.

The leaders or facilitators of groups with social change goals have several tasks. One is to ensure that such goals are realistic and to contribute their knowledge and experience to help the group in setting and pursuing its goals. A second is to place responsibility with group members for decisions, action and support, from which confidence in their own abilities and efforts may increase.

Another set of aims may be defined as group-centred. In residential care (Mullender, 1990), the aim may be to improve quality of life for individuals and the whole community, to maximise independence but also mutual support. Elsewhere, the objectives of the group are derived from problems experienced by the group prior to or outside the workers' involvement with it. The group is used as a therapeutic resource, that is, the resources of the group members and groupworkers are used to achieve the group's objectives. Thus, for sexually abused children, a group can increase their self-esteem and provide an opportunity to share experiences and feelings, from which young people can feel empowered (Lebacq and Shah, 1989). Breton (1991) suggests working with marginalised populations to create a competence-promoting environment, providing nurture and optimal challenges, learning and consciousness-raising. Such groupwork activity enables people to regain control of their lives, to appreciate how socio-economic and political forces have combined to contribute to their individual and group difficulties, and to evaluate their strengths. Similarly, Lee (1991) includes as empowering group-centred aims:

● To improve transactions between people and their contexts to enhance adaptive capabilities and improve their environments.
● To create resources.
● To restructure situations.
● To promote people's competence, identity and autonomy, and to reduce powerlessness.

A group may act together for effectiveness, using its collective intellectual and emotional resources to achieve social change goals or to demonstrate how others can act helpfully towards members. Put another way, a group may use its collective power to challenge stereotypes held by others. Equally the objective might be to establish a self-help forum where the goals might include enriching the lives of the members or improving relationships with peers.

Another cluster of aims may be defined as individual-centred. They may take the form of helping members understand and develop the resources to live with, lessen or eradicate personal problems of social functioning which cause them to experience their lives as unsatisfactory, difficult to manage, lacking in quality or unacceptable to others (Brown *et al.*, 1982). Thus, the aim may be expressed as the achievement of insight. It may be defined as the exploration of feelings and the acquisition of understanding of their own and others' motivation behind behaviour, for example about offending (Caddick, 1991), and of self-defeating ways of dealing with problems. Alternatively, the aim may be defined in terms of individual development, often referred to as treatment. Here the effort may be directed towards developing new ways of behaving to overcome obstacles to social development and growth, with the group providing opportunities to rehearse these. The emphasis may be on narrowing the gap between potential and actual functioning, for example in a group aiming to prepare young people for school. Or again, the aim may be specified as providing missing life experiences or enabling members to adopt new roles to improve their social functioning. The emphasis is on individual change, the focus being problems which members share but experience individually outside the group. Whether described as aiming for increased self-esteem, improved capacity to relate to others, or increased ability to use personal skills and resources, the objective is personality change, either behavioural, emotional or attitudinal.

For example, Mullender (1996) describes how groupwork can challenge the minimisation and denial used by men who abuse. Bensted and colleagues (1994) focus on men's patterns of offending and the culture of masculinity into which they have been socialised, in order to help them understand aspects of themselves as men and to broaden their understanding of the need for personal change. Mistry (1989) combines individual, group and social change aims with women offenders, to enable them to take control of their lives, to address offending in its context of their socio-economic status and position in a patriarchal society, to challenge each other and to build their own support system. Her groupwork programme focuses, therefore, on group dynamics and on external problems that encroach on the lives of group members.

Another task, then, for practitioners intending to run or facilitate a group is to formulate a general aim or purpose. Having identified the need, problems or circumstances that might become a focus or target, what is the group's main purpose? Are there any secondary purposes? These broad aims may be a starting point for interacting with actual or potential members. They may be modified and sharpened into specific objectives for the group as a whole and for individual members in the light of referrals. Further refinement comes with a group being formed, discussions with members, and the resources actually available in the group. The rationale for defining initial purposes is that, if the leaders or facilitators are unclear, they may give confused messages to the group on the degree of participation required and on acceptable or potential goals. Furthermore, the more the groupworkers are able to establish clear, initial purposes, the better they will be able to facilitate discussion among members of their view of the group's purpose and of whether to accept the offer of a group and/or the intervention of social (care) workers. They will be better placed to make alternative or supplementary suggestions regarding aims and to consider whether the group will satisfy their perception of their needs and situation.

Theoretical frameworks, styles of work and leadership

In this process of formulating the type of and purpose for a group, and later in understanding the group's dynamics and guiding their interaction with the group, practitioners will be influenced by particular theoretical frameworks and styles of work or leadership.

Social workers may use a psychological theoretical base. This may take the form of a psychodynamic understanding and interpretation of the group, for example using the framework that the group's work task may be hindered by emotional drives, unconscious basic assumptions of fight–flight, pairing and dependency (Bion, 1961). An alternative psychodynamic framework for understanding members' experiences and group behaviour is focal conflict theory (Whitaker, 2001). The key here is what is avoided: anxiety or a dreaded situation. Solutions adopted by individuals and the group may be restrictive, to limit exploration, or enabling, to encourage analysis. These solutions may be detected in the group's mood, culture, cohesiveness, relationships and work. A key theoretical consideration here for analysis is how individuals' childhoods and later experiences are recreated as emotional tensions in the context of the group and its leader/facilitator. Methods used will, therefore, aim to identify and resolve old disturbing conflicts by bringing them into awareness.

Behavioural groupwork draws on the principles of behavioural psychology and is characterised by applying learning theory in the group situation. A wide variety of behavioural techniques can be used, such as homework, role rehearsal and positive reinforcement programmes. Social skills groupwork is closely related to behavioural groupwork but is more task-orientated and concentrates on micro-skills, including cognitive skills that individuals may lack. For instance, inappropriate eye contact in interview situations may be a particular problem, which may be overcome using group methods of rehearsal, modelling and reinforcement to help people develop the desired behaviour.

Humanistic methods, while also derived from psychodynamic understanding, emphasise human emotional development and the power of the group to facilitate the release of feelings and the achievement of personal growth. Methods used include group exercises to encourage openness and self-revelation, effective communication, and social and personal development, such as role plays, exercises, trust games, art and drama. Once again, the aim is to encourage people to set aside old ways of being and behaving, to resolve unfinished business, and thereby to release energy for new relationships.

Social workers may use a sociological theoretical base to inform their practice, emphasising a structural analysis of members' difficulties or circumstances rather than locating difficulties within the members themselves. They may emphasise power issues and the labelling process, with a group providing the opportunity for changing roles and interactions between members, and between them and outsiders. They may be particularly interested in natural or preexisting groups, such as gangs, looking at their nature and function.

Social workers may use a systems approach, that is, viewing the group as a system, each member as a subsystem within it, and the group as part of a wider network or supra-system. The utility of this framework can be seen in the complex patterns of relatedness, or mosaics (Brown, 1990), in residential and day care settings. One task for groupworkers here will be to understand how different parts of the mosaic interact, how individuals move between different groups, and how organisational, group and individual pressures and processes can distort relationships and communication. Group-workers may focus on the input and output of the system or on the effect on the group and individual members of the outside environment and on the relationships between individuals and sub-groups within the group. With a systemic perspective groupworkers view each system as having a purpose or goal. This is discovered through formulating and testing hypotheses, which are neither true nor false but more or less useful, and used as a basis for intervention without reference to truth. Data are collected that will validate, disconfirm or modify each hypothesis. Hypothesising enables groupworkers to track interactional patterns both within the group and between it and systems outside the group, to involve every member and to establish how the group's organisation and behaviour fit together. The rationale is that individual change can only occur after a change in the system.

Groupworkers may bring a feminist perspective, which conventional groupwork theory has overlooked (Cohen and Mullender, 2003). Working with women offenders (Mistry, 1989) using this framework challenges sexism within agency policy and practice. It views women's offences through the lens of their socio-economic position in a patriarchal society. It challenges the view of women as subordinate and promotes their ability to take control of their lives. It emphasises the elimination of false dichotomies (Groves and Schondel, 1997/98), such as between group members and group-workers. It renames and reconceptualises issues: the personal becomes political and structural, with a focus on oppressive social divisions and power. Values of equity, reciprocity in communication, inclusiveness and unity in diversity characterise this approach (Lee, 1999). The methods used aim to challenge the use of stereotypes, to raise consciousness by sharing experiences of oppression and gendered practices that limit individual growth and social change (Cohen and Mullender, 2003), and to develop assertiveness skills in relation to people and situations experienced as oppressive. There are clear parallels here with anti-racist practice and with anti-oppressive practice. They also focus on social divisions, power and oppression, and involve an awareness of power structures both internal and external to the group. Once again, the key aim is for groupwork to transform personal issues into common concerns, and to facilitate member-led action that changes both personal psychology and the social environment within which individuals and groups reside.

All these theoretical models have something to offer to understanding groups and to shaping groupwork practice. Indeed, an eclectic frame of reference, which draws carefully from these models, is commonly used (Brown *et al.*, 1982). It may provide greater flexibility in response to the multiple causation of members' difficulties and the many influences on the group's processes. However, groupworkers must properly think through an eclectic approach. Is the combination of ideas being used compatible with their values? Is it coherent in terms of its analysis and the methods derived therefrom? Is it responsive to the needs of the group?

The purpose in identifying theoretical frameworks is fourfold. A lack of clarity can create confusion for members and leaders/facilitators about what the group can and cannot achieve. Theory makes sense of and informs practice. Theoretical perspectives enable groupworkers to understand behaviours and provide frameworks for what action to take. Their response will, at least partly, be determined by their knowledge and beliefs about how behaviour and needs may be understood (Fatout, 1997/98). Accordingly, groupworkers must cultivate open awareness or a meta position. This is because any lens cannot incorporate all experience (Nosko and Breton, 1997/98). Equally, it can distort. Explanatory frameworks, and the techniques that flow from them, can betray assumptions, for instance about male violence towards women (Mullender, 1996). Groups designed to challenge men's myths and denials may actually make men more dangerous, or dangerous in different ways, because the frameworks and/or methods used do not focus sufficiently on intra- and interpersonal relationship change, or on men's individual and social dominance over women.

Second, theoretical frameworks will shape the methods practitioners use in a group and may lead them away from enabling the group to pursue other aims. For instance, a psychodynamically oriented groupworker is unlikely to emphasise social change goals which, however, may feel relevant to members. Third, frameworks can make sense of the group's dynamics. Finally, different models construct the groupworker's role differently – as leaders or as facilitators. Thus, self-directed groupwork envisages practitioners not as group leaders but as group facilitators (Ward and Mullender, 1991), assisting members to set their own goals and to take action collectively. They often work, then, within a preexisting group leadership structure and negotiate the boundaries of their own role.

Therefore, another task for practitioners is to familiarise themselves with the theoretical models available and how these concepts shape how they operate and influence their styles of work and leadership.

---

putting into practice: drawing on theory

➢ What frames of reference do I use in my approach to groupwork?
➢ What do I understand by the term 'group dynamics'? What understanding do I have about the dynamics of behaviour in and between groups?
➢ What theoretical studies have influenced my thinking about groupwork?
➢ What is my preferred way of working in groups?
➢ What do I see as the tasks and responsibilities of groupworkers?
➢ What style is most congenial to me? Will this enable me to achieve the broad aims of the group?
➢ Do I see myself as determining the group's aims or is this to be shared with members or are they taking on this task?

Source: Hodge (1985).

Conclusion

This chapter has presented a definition of a group and a classification of types and purposes of groups. It has suggested that groupworkers have several tasks, namely to consider what type of group they are working with, what its aims are, and what theoretical frameworks may helpfully shape their practice. In the next chapter this thinking will be taken further by working through the stages in planning a group. This is necessary if groupwork is to have its extraordinary impact on people's lives (Doel and Sawdon, 1999a), to be a source of empowerment rather than a site of continuing inequality to people's detriment (McLeod, 2003), and to enhance the quality of the service provided by agencies.

4 | Planning the group

Introduction

Having researched and understood the need for work with groups, and having surveyed types of groups and broad aims, the next step is to devote time to planning. This may involve formation of a group or practitioners negotiating to join a preexisting group. Whichever, future effectiveness of any group depends on thorough preparation and planning, which are complex tasks. To illustrate this complexity, how should groupworkers respond to contacts from group members between sessions? If co-working, how should they divide their tasks? When planning to form a group, how should members be selected and what should groupworkers do if too many or too few referrals are received? In newly formed or natural groups, what is the interrelationship between the group's task and size? If this interrelationship is misconstrued, some members may be left uninvolved or under-involved in the group's tasks, which may prevent the group attaining its goals. Alternatively, the group may have inadequate resources (knowledge, skills, time) for the task it faces. Finally, with any group how might group-workers negotiate their authority in a way that will not confuse members or result in conflicts and tensions being played out in the group to the frustration of its tasks?

So, time for planning is essential (Doel and Sawdon, 2001). Lebacq and Shah (1989) recommend that groupworkers consider 'what if?' questions, that is, anticipate and develop strategies for managing possible member behaviours or scenarios. Springer and colleagues (1999) offer one example of inadequate planning and, indeed, of consideration about group size and needs. Groupworkers had not visited the rooms to be used, or screened potential members, or thought through goal-setting. Neither the workers nor the children who were group members had any idea what they were getting into, the latter because they had not previously met the workers or been given any information about the group. If insufficient time or thought is given to planning, groupworkers and members may find that their plans are too ambitious or too confusing and threatening. Alternatively, leadership or facilitation may be experienced by everyone as muddled and uncertain, with a consequent loss of confidence in groupworkers' skills and abilities.

Additional complexity derives from the question of who plans. When forming groups, especially if groupworkers are prepared to share ownership of the group through involvement of actual or potential members, inclusiveness may confirm for members that the group will be a useful experience. Inclusivity may enhance members' self-esteem, generate ideas and confirm or extend prior understanding of people's needs, laying the foundation for future creative and collaborative working.

There is a balance to be found here. Groupworkers should not underestimate people's capacity for sustained and creative involvement. Indeed, applying a strengths and empowerment model (Nosko and Breton, 1997/98) means, in relation to power, identifying members' competence, assuming strengths, and seeing those involved as teachers, whose explanations can help us all to understand. Adopting this model means that central to planning and preparation are listening and learning what people bring, tuning in and leading or facilitating the development of content and process. The group generates its structure and determines its focus by sharing ideas about the topic area and options for how to address it. However, when working with marginalised populations (Breton, 1991) or with people who have internalised oppression, requests for participation should not exceed the practical and emotional resources which they feel able to offer. Nonetheless, involvement demonstrates a concern to revalue and empower rather than to reinforce marginalisation and powerlessness. It is consistent with anti-oppressive or emancipatory practice. Besides the ethical considerations here, there are also the pragmatic. Beginning planning with decisions, or exercising control over planning, may lead groupworkers to consider the wrong questions, may undermine potential for collaborative learning, and may reduce the likelihood of ultimate acceptance of group goals.

So, actual or potential members' voices and perspectives should be heard and the greatest possible involvement in planning and self-determination promoted. Groupworkers should engage in an open dialogue rather than prematurely close off options by deciding about membership, leadership and other issues (Mullender and Ward, 1989). Groupworkers, therefore, need to be clear about their own power base and how this changes as negotiation about content and process unfolds. This chapter, then, focuses on the membership of the group, while Chapter 5 covers its operation and factors external to it. Throughout this process groupworkers should acknowledge the distribution of power within and outside the group and be clear about their own values, especially in terms of what is non-negotiable from the standpoint of practising anti-oppressive principles. This is the opportunity for partnership in action, recognising the roles of members or potential clients in shaping decisions on frequency, venue and duration, and in challenging agency policies and perspectives. It is where groupwork can begin to be truly transformative.

Group membership

Counteracting discrimination

When considering questions relating to a group's membership, it is helpful if groupworkers are clear on the type of group they wish to conduct or interact with, and on the structure most useful to potential members. It is clearly preferable to conduct preparatory discussions with members in order to explore the possibilities and any preferences that participants may have. It is effective practice too to keep planning decisions under review, being prepared to reconsider particular questions when this might facilitate group dynamics or process and/or achievement of the group's aims.

Throughout, groupworkers should reflect on how structural discrimination, whether racism, sexism, disablism, heterosexism or ageism, is being imported into or reflected in a group. This may be because groupworkers have not considered their own cultural assumptions or paid sufficient attention to acknowledging and validating differences in people's experiences. The environment surrounding the group – its physical setting, its resources, its staffing, its procedures and policies – may reflect and reinforce rather than challenge discrimination. For example, it may fail to promote black people's perspectives or to recognise that black women may experience the negative impact of membership of more than one social division.

putting into practice: power audit

> What are group members' sources of power?
> What are groupworkers' sources of power?
> How can any power imbalance in planning groupwork be acknowledged?
> What empowers and disempowers you to practise groupwork anti-oppressively in your agency?
> What can you do to reduce the disempowering factors and to maximise the empowering factors?

putting into practice: reflection

> If you were a service user, how safe would it feel to:
> * provide feedback
> * claim rights
> * complain, challenge or question?

What would make you feel this?

> How encouraging would you, as a service user, see the agency in terms of:
> * partnership
> * listening for feedback
> * acknowledging social divisions and their overlap
> * enabling people to assert their rights
> * enabling people to challenge discrimination?

What would make you feel this?

putting into practice: removing barriers

How will service users know that 'race', ethnicity, gender, sexuality, language, culture, disability and poverty are taken into consideration in (a) information-giving about the group, (b) consideration of membership, (c) the actual groupwork service provided? How will service users know that groupworkers are working, or wanting to work, in partnership with them?

These exercises highlight that anti-oppressive groupwork practice requires a personal and an organisational commitment. Personal commitment was discussed in Chapter 2 but it must be underpinned by an organisational value base that endorses this approach and seeks to empower workers and members to achieve it.

The organisational contribution to anti-oppressive groupwork practice includes explicit policies which create a safe space in which questioning is encouraged, for example of how power is used or relationships are defined. Power relationships are openly and squarely addressed, and the mandates for the work, and their effects, openly discussed. It includes support groups for practitioners and a physical environment that conveys empowering messages through the resources it provides. It focuses on the impact of structural factors and the experience of oppression and social divisions in terms of people's perceptions of their ability to act, their experiences of alienation and/or isolation, and their expectations.

The personal as well as organisational commitment is to manage power in a way that empowers (Preston-Shoot, 1995). Various types of inequality and oppression permeate social (care) work and therefore groupwork, such that reflexivity should be a constant. At an intrapersonal level this entails a readiness to scrutinise personal bias, values, use of power and the potential to oppress; to explore the implications for and effect on practice of personal experience of and involvement in sources of inequality. At an interpersonal level it entails practice that builds upon people's strengths, experiences and perspectives, upon recognition of diversity in experiences of power and inequality, and of the interaction of multiple oppressions. It entails a willingness to embrace other people's perspectives and to understand the connections between their experiences, context and behaviour. Power is centre stage when planning work – who sets the agenda and the parameters for working together? At a structural level it requires skills in raising issues about policy and structures, about how oppression and, for example, gendered assumptions may manifest themselves or be reinforced in service delivery. It is coupled with a critical ability to discern when and how to do so. This involves asking questions about the exercise of power, about socially constructed and internalised attitudes, reflected in practice assumptions and procedures. It requires an ability to avoid collusive, authoritarian or defensive practice with colleagues and service users, and an ability to empower users not to accept agency practice uncritically (Preston-Shoot, 1995).

Central then is a principle of co-learning, reference and negotiation, rather than deference or acquiescence by others. This principle underpins the attempt to maximise people's control of defining the issues to be addressed and decisions to be taken, and then of taking action and decision-making. This is done through the provision of information, support to empower people when they are faced with the unfamiliar, clarification of non-negotiable items, and scrutinising what proposed interventions might be 'saying' about power, powerlessness and the 'playing out' of social divisions. In defining work goals, the assumption is that people are competent (Mullender, 1991) and that the groupworker's role is one of negotiated facilitation.

Open or closed membership?

Traditionally this has been seen to depend very much on the purpose and type of group. Thus, frequent changes in membership may not unduly disrupt social groups. However, task- or goal-oriented groups may require a period of stability in order to develop and operate as a group and not to lose focus and continuity by having to deal with the feelings and fantasies surrounding the loss of members or the introduction of newcomers. Tribe (1997/98) suggests that variable membership may slow down or affect group life; Schneewind (1996) that relationships develop gradually when membership fluctuates. It may be that a closed group will promote cohesion and trust, and provide security for members who initially are apprehensive or lacking in confidence. However, a small group may cease to be viable if closed and if more than a few members leave or fail to attend regularly. One way to try to avoid this scenario is by operating an open then closed cycle, enabling members to take some time in deciding whether to commit and to ensure optimum size.

Where members are chosen on a homogeneous basis, that is, where they have problems, needs or experiences in common, a closed group may enable it to gel fairly quickly. However, the learning opportunities in an open-ended or heterogeneous group should not be undervalued. Open groups may offer greater flexibility to reconstitute and redefine themselves within the spirit of their original general purpose (Henry, 1988; Schneewind, 1996), and member involvement in open groups may be greater (Hopmeyer and Werk, 1993). Indeed, assumptions about open groups should be revisited (Henry, 1988) since they are not necessarily problematic or less cohesive (Mullender and Ward, 1989). Rather, as Breton (1991) and Henry (1988) identify, open groups may:

● Allow people concerned about commitment or about relationship intensity to enter at their own pace.
● Allow marginalised populations to influence the group and enable the group to influence these communities by openness about definition of required tasks.
● Reduce apprehension about further marginalisation by minimising rigidity about who is inside and who outside.
● Respect that people learn and grow in different ways; for some it may be particularly important for them to keep control of what and how they learn.
● Retain continuity by having a core purpose or goal that provides a frame of reference, by building a history and culture that is passed on as membership changes, and by increasing the resources (especially people) from which members may learn.
● Facilitate cohesion if members and facilitators/leaders negotiate timing of entry and exit according to the stage a group has reached.
● Facilitate cohesion where the same groupworkers, whether practitioner or peer leaders or facilitators, provide continuity, giving particular attention to enabling the group to manage the impact of changes and fluctuations in membership on the group's identity, programme and work.

Where groupworkers are working with a preexisting group or a given population, such as a tenants' group or groups in residential settings, it may not indeed be possible to maintain the same membership over time. One possible response to this is to operate a closed/open/closed cycle. Adding new members at defined points if some individuals have left allows throughput when groupwork as a resource to meet felt or assessed needs is in high demand. It allows people to control their own participation levels and meeting of their needs (Hopmeyer and Werk, 1993) but it also gives the group time to develop and focus on its purposes.

If the group is closed but attendance is likely to be erratic, or if the group has open membership throughout, groupworkers can minimise the extent to which this might undermine the group's effectiveness by careful programming. Each session may be an event in itself rather than part of a linked or developmental progression.

Number of members?

Traditionally this too has been seen as dependent on the purpose and type of group. For example, where the aim is to enable members to verbalise their feelings, a small group may be less threatening or, alternatively, may lead members to feel pressurised into describing their feelings and to become defensive. On the other hand, a large group can be a setting where reticent members can hide or where some members are uninvolved or under-involved in the group's task. There are, however, techniques for involving members and for raising issues in larger groups, such as the use of small groupings followed by feedback, and creative cloudbursts on flip charts. Nonetheless, any decision concerning the group's size should consider the resources and personalities of the potential members, for which members completing a self-audit may prove useful.

Conventional wisdom concerning groups with therapeutic purposes recommends an optimum size of around eight members, suggesting that this facilitates task orientation, expression of disagreement and social interaction. Groupworkers may choose to recruit several additional members to allow for subsequent dropouts. However, whether the aim is individual or community change, a group of this size may or may not have sufficient resources in terms of members' skills in task and/or process roles, such as the generation of ideas. There may be insufficient experience or energy to be creative or to offer alternative methods of tackling personal difficulties.

Conventional wisdom suggests that the smaller the group, the greater the likelihood that one-to-one interaction between members or with the groupworkers will develop rather than interaction as a group. Further, there is a greater likelihood that intimacy will exist but also an increased possibility of disintegration because of absence or withdrawal from the group. However, groupworker or member facilitation skills may promote the development of group interaction in a small group and of intimacy in a larger group. Conventional wisdom also suggests that the larger the group, the greater the likelihood of subgroup formation or of a small grouping being very active, surrounded by silent onlookers. In very large groups, freedom of expression may be reduced. Once again, however, some people may feel more comfortable in larger groups, and member or groupworker skills may enable subgroupings to work effectively for the benefit of the larger group.

Therefore, in considering size, the task is to create the optimum conditions for the group to achieve its purposes. Accordingly, groupworkers should define size in relation to the group's aims and objectives, and the skills required to achieve them. Two further difficulties commonly arise here. First, particularly in groups that have formed naturally, groupworkers may have to work with a group which they consider too small or large for the tasks it is attempting to accomplish. One response to this is to discuss with the group whether and how to encourage other people to join or how the group is to structure its work to enable each member to be involved. Second, where social workers are forming groups, the number of eligible members may be small. It is tempting, but probably inadvisable, to run the group when the number of members is felt to be too small for the tasks envisaged.

Workers' clients as members of the group?

There are several advantages to having own clients in a group. Social (care) workers will have a greater awareness of their clients' needs and an opportunity to use existing positive relationships to provide initial reassurance for them within the group. Social workers will see how family members function outside their family. This may provide a more effective integration of groupwork with other services being offered.

However, these may not turn out to be advantages. Practitioners and clients have to adapt to the change of format and roles, and the presence of own clients in a group can create difficulties of confidentiality, exclusive relationships or factionalism, resentment and rivalry (Yalom, 1995). Unresolved transference issues may leak into the group when clients have had previous individual help from a groupworker (Fitzsimmons and Levy, 1996). As regards confidentiality, how should groupworkers respond to information given in a group about people outside it, or outside the group about people within it? This is one aspect of a potential difficulty in keeping the roles and tasks of the contexts separate. This may be seen in members confiding in the groupworker but not in the group, using the group as an individual session with an audience. Or it may be highlighted through members discussing problems which do not relate to the group's task, perhaps raising issues that can be followed up only outside the group. Moreover, other family members with whom the social worker interacts may feel excluded or threatened by the client's membership of a group run by their social worker. These feelings may interfere either with the family work or with the client's membership of the group. Both client and groupworker also face the issue of what information or progress in respect of the group is to be shared with these significant others. An early negotiation of a protocol on what information will or will not be shared, in what circumstances, may prove helpful.

Nor are all relationships between caseworkers and clients positive. Negative past relationships and experiences might be brought into the group, reducing its effectiveness and the potential of relationships formed within it. Members may find the group difficult because of disappointed expectations that it is not identical to other contexts in which they meet with their social worker. Own clients as group members might generate conflict between those who have social workers and those who do not, or may create a situation where members relate more to their social worker than to the group or co-worker.

Groupworkers can use a variety of responses in these instances. Within the group they can bring other members into the conversation or use the co-worker more actively with clients of the other leader/facilitator. They might direct members' comments into the group and decline to be drawn into an individual relationship during the session. It may be appropriate, especially where it seems to be creating difficulties, to discuss with members their feelings about the presence of the groupworkers' clients in the group. Prior to beginning the group it is useful to discuss with potential members and significant others the implications of membership for the member, their family and the social (care) worker, what is to be shared about the group and how this will be done. Finally, co-workers should share their knowledge of potential members to ensure that each is able to take a full part in the group and avoid a secondary role.

Selection

When groupworkers propose to engage with preexisting groups, as in residential care, day care or youth groups, it is inappropriate to think in terms of selection from referrals. Here, whether or not there is any fluidity of membership, groupworkers may meet with people beforehand to give information, to discuss what problems or issues concern members and how they understand them, and to explore how working as a group might enable effective action to be taken (Mullender and Ward, 1989).

Where practitioners are forming a group, how are members to be selected? On the basis of experience of working with lesbian survivors of incest, Groves and Schondel (1997/98) concluded that it was better to avoid selecting couples for the group in order to avoid such dynamics as a united pair against the group. Lebacq and Shah (1989), working with sexually abused children, discovered that it was advisable to consider the quality and dynamics of sibling relationships prior to any decision about their inclusion in the same group. There are gender implications behind possible selection options. Weinstein (1994) observed that women tend to use groups for support, validation, strength and a growing sense of personal awareness. Hopmeyer and Werk (1993) found that women share feelings while men problem-solve and gather information. Lebacq and Shah (1989) concluded that the focus of an all-boys group would involve exploring non-abusive role models more fully in order to decrease any potential identification with the abuser, whereas that of an all-girls group would prioritise how to avoid victim roles and develop assertiveness skills. Gender can affect what people want and how they respond to oppression. In mixed groups women may find themselves expected to nurture and support men, with their own needs for support, nurturing and self-disclosure submerged or significantly impeded again (Mistry, 1989).

Similar issues emerge in respect of 'race'. Lebacq and Shah (1989) found that a mixed group of young children in terms of 'race' and gender resulted in there being too many variables, with the result that the impact of abuse and racism on children was not properly addressed. They concluded that a group composed solely of black children would enable greater depth of work on their experience of racism and its impacts.

In relation to all social divisions, then, familiar factors may impede necessary levels of openness to confront, understand and work through issues of power and oppression arising from such differences (Kohli, 1993). Without care, group composition may replicate social divisions and reinforce inequalities. Thus, groupworkers should consider how group composition will enable the experience of oppression, and the interconnected impact of social divisions (Cohen, 2003), to be challenged.

Selection, then, is an intricate exercise. Unlikely combinations may work well, carefully selected groups may not. An ideal composition is not found easily. The attributes viewed as essential for membership will depend on the group's objectives which, therefore, should be outlined before leaders consider questions of membership and selection. Indeed, with both preexisting groups and groups being formed, and where potential membership is the totality of persons in a setting, groupworkers, and members where appropriate and possible, need to reflect on what characteristics, roles and skills are required amongst the membership (Hodge, 1985). In other words, for whom is the group intended? Who might benefit from or contribute to the type of group planned? What resources within individual members, and the membership overall, are essential and/or desirable?

Answers to these questions will depend on the group's aims and the specific cluster of needs, problems or issues that are the target for intervention. Thus, age, gender, relationship status, socioeconomic circumstances, severity of problems, geographical location and specific personality qualities may or may not form part of the selection criteria (Hodge, 1985). For example, a group may find the aim of breaking down isolation or establishing a self-help group unobtainable if members live too far apart. Likewise, in a discussion group, the ability to verbalise and to talk openly about emotional and social concerns may be crucial. In a group with social action goals, it is probably important that potential members can access the resources for collective action and have similar experiences concerning the target for intervention. It is necessary too that they are not so preoccupied with their individual difficulties or situations that they have little motivation for a cooperative effort.

Leaders should avoid any composition that isolates one individual. For instance, it is unwise to form a group consisting of one offender and the remainder non-offenders, or one man and the remainder women. This is because the isolated person may feel both exposed and vulnerable. Additionally, the individual tends not to be seen as such but as representative of their grouping and thus risks being stereotyped by the others (Whitaker, 2001).

It is useful to think in terms of descriptive and behavioural characteristics. Descriptive characteristics include age, gender, relationship status, occupation and involvement with the social work agency. Behavioural characteristics include ways in which the individuals act or may be expected to behave in the group. A third category is situational characteristics: the problems, difficulties, circumstances and emotional or social concerns that members have as individuals. This leads into consideration of heterogeneity and homogeneity, that is, the balance of difference and commonality.

Brown (1997) suggests that homogeneity facilitates stability and cohesion, promoting satisfying interpersonal relationships, while heterogeneity introduces vitality and increases resources for problem-solving and change. Rice and Goodman (1992), working with support groups for older people, identify the task as being to balance the diversity of resources (coping responses and perspectives) offered by heterogeneity with the enhanced intimacy or cohesiveness from homogeneity. They suggest that homogeneity of concern, capacity to tolerate anxiety, and vulnerability can facilitate group cohesion and the development of open and interactive groups marked by empathy, the ability to tolerate conflict and disclosure, while heterogeneity around patterns of coping can maximise the learning opportunities available. Pease (2003), however, observes that commonality can also promote collusion rather than transformation. Cohen (2003) cautions against seeing women only as a homogeneous group dichotomised from men. Similar caution about attributing homogeneity attaches to service users and carers. This underlines the complexity of social divisions. Thiara (2003) sees differences and commonalities across various axes, with the result that groupworkers should ask several questions:

● Is what is common likely to enable collective action?
● How do people construct their specific experiences?
● Where can difference be used to assist the development of a collective identity?

● Is what the group wants to achieve a more useful place to begin than who members are in terms of social divisions?

With these caveats in mind, if the purpose of the group is support, homogeneous characteristics may be important since this may help the group to gel. If the group's objective is personality change, a homogeneous composition, especially of behavioural characteristics, might encourage resistance and defensiveness in a group or reduce the range of choices and experiences open to members. Here a heterogeneous composition in terms of personality characteristics may prove more beneficial. Where the aim is personality change, groupworkers do not want members who are so similar that one solution is reinforced in the group. Nor, however, do they want members who are so different that they find interaction difficult. This is not the same as saying that groupworkers should avoid selecting people with common problems. Many successful groups are run for people with similar problems since commonality fosters acceptance and the realisation that they are not unique. However, what is important is that they do not share the same approaches in dealing with their problems. For example, in bereavement groups Hopmeyer and Werk (1993) found that homogeneity to the problem but heterogeneity to relationships to the deceased worked best.

However, should groupworkers select members? If handled insensitively, the process of selection could reinforce social exclusion, reproduce feelings of powerlessness or hopelessness, and strengthen negative impressions of professional practice. However, not all potential members are able to function in every type of group. A sensitive way of handling selection is to use referral forms and to offer the group to prospective members since this requires the participants to be clear about and to discuss their aims and perceptions. Referral forms fulfil several purposes. They assist everyone in being clear about their aims and expectations and help groupworkers to be specific in their planning and presentation of the group and in selecting members. They also provide a baseline, an initial measure for evaluating the outcome of the group and a starting point for negotiating a contract, specific aims and a programme for the group with members.

Nonetheless, groupworkers may wish to avoid being too specific about clients who might benefit from the group. This vagueness in selection criteria might be based on a lack of faith in identifying suitable members or on a fear that specificity will discourage referrals, which are difficult enough to obtain anyway. However, to a large extent, the formed group's ultimate effectiveness will be determined by care at this stage.

In designing a referral form, groupworkers need to decide what they want to know and what questions they want to ask. For example, do groupworkers need to know about home circumstances, school performance and the member's family relationships? Reflective of partnership, groupworkers should provide a description of the group they are proposing, which should include its possible aims, length, timing of sessions and suggested rules on confidentiality. Furthermore, groupworkers should request that referrers complete the referral form with the potential member and, to this end, the questions should be phrased in such a way that the service user is responding. In addition, a brief statement should be provided concerning how the referral form will be used.

Useful questions might include:

- What do you want or hope to gain from the group?
- How do you see this group fitting in with other services you are receiving?
- What do you think are your main difficulties?
- What have you tried to do about them?
- What particularly concerns or worries you?
- What would you like to be different?
- What do you think are the good things in your life?
- What skills, strengths and abilities would you bring to this group?
- What does your social worker see as your main difficulties?
- What does your social worker see as your main skills and strengths?
- What does your social worker hope you will gain from the group?
- What problems have you and your social worker been working on?
- How does your social worker feel that the group will help you both with the problems you have been working on?
- What might you find difficult in a group?

● What are the attitudes of your family/significant others to the group?
● How keen are you *really* to join the group?

Offering the group to prospective members

---

putting into practice: reflecting on referral

Imagine you have been referred to a group. What anxieties and questions might you have? What might you be worried about? What would you want to know? What would you experience as empowering and disempowering?

In your groupwork practice, how do you respond to the feedback from the answers to these questions?

Interestingly, groupworkers in one survey (Doel and Sawdon, 2001) rated as relatively unimportant offering the group to individuals who might be interested. However, a personal offer, whether to join a group being formed or to use a preexisting group for a specific suggested purpose, can be crucial to success because of the dynamics that groupworkers can create to enable people to join. Thus, positive outcomes are more likely when groupworkers demonstrate an approach recognised as legitimate by members (Hayden *et al.*, 1999). Offering the group helps to deal with sources of reluctance (Behroozi, 1992) and with any felt reservations about participating (Manor, 1988) which, if unaddressed, would probably impact on attendance or group process.

---

putting into practice: offering a group

You are a groupworker and this is the individual's first contact with you. What indication would you have given by letter or telephone beforehand about the reasons for the meeting? What would you want to cover that would provide a sense of the group, your practice, and your employing agency?

Rehearse the points you want to cover with a colleague in order to reflect on what works well and what might work better in this introduction.

It is useful if groupworkers meet potential members before the group begins. To begin with, the group's effectiveness depends on members being able to function in the type of group being envisaged. Even when this has been established, members may be ambivalent about the group, even showing high levels of defensiveness, resistance and denial (Shulman, 1988). They may be suspicious or confused about the group's purpose, the roles that the groupworkers will adopt, and the nature of the participation expected of them. They may feel that they have nothing to offer, or less to give than others have. They may feel sceptical about its likely achievements and impact or, reflective of internalised oppression, feel pessimistic about the attainability of change. They may anticipate being isolated or being uncomfortable with the expression of either emotion or disagreement. The stress of joining or uncertainty about the group's goals may lead them to be defensive, especially since similarities between members will only become apparent once the group has met. In a group where membership is to be compulsory or where the choice to join is coloured by the approval of significant others, a strong possibility exists of non-compliance and aggression, which may be seen in superficial cooperation, silence or acting out. In any event, potential members may have had negative experiences previously of professionals and their use of positional authority.

Preparatory interviews enable the groupworkers and potential members to recognise and discuss feelings and problems occasioned by the suggestion of working together. They can explore motivation (Doel and Sawdon, 1999b), for even those whose membership is voluntary might have preferred not to be eligible. They may not want to encounter or expose feelings of perceived failure, or be seen as incompetent or uncertain. They may fear loss of self-respect. Perceptions of coercion can be explored (Behroozi, 1992). Almost certainly this will have to be repeated in the first group meetings if the work is not to be sabotaged by non-attendance, superficial cooperation or uncooperative silence. However, preparatory interviews do provide the opportunity for members to discuss their reservations about the group or problems in taking up membership. They can make practical and emotional preparations (Doel and Sawdon, 1999a). They enable participants to assess the extent to which they share a similar definition of problems or aims, and to ensure that false expectations are not raised. Groupworkers can clarify the limits of their own and the agency's commitment.

Before offering the group, groupworkers have several tasks. They need to decide how to present the group's aims realistically and clearly to avoid raising false expectations and in a manner that anticipates members' likely concerns, fears or uncertainties. They must be clear about what the group may achieve and what it might involve for members. Another task is to decide how to discuss the group's purpose in a manner that will enable members to match this with their perceptions of their needs and to assimilate the rationale for the group. Finally, groupworkers should present what they believe they can offer the group, using their personal profiles that are discussed later. Where possible, co-workers should offer the group to members, or engage in negotiation with a preexisting group, jointly since this prepares members for a triadic rather than dyadic relationship.

Preparatory interviews are concerned not just with convincing people of the benefits of working together but also with enabling them to transform this information into envisaging the group as something for themselves (Manor, 1988). Preparatory discussions are a two-way process of clarification. What is discussed will depend on the nature and purpose of the group. For instance, in a group where personal difficulties might be shared, it is important to assess how willing prospective members are to share their thoughts and feelings with others. Information given in the referral form provides a useful beginning for exploring members' expectations of the group and whether the leaders/facilitators and potential members are out of step or share sufficient common ground. It provides too an opportunity for developing what members would like the group to do for them and for clarifying their difficulties, concerns and strengths. It is from this information that groupworkers and members can assess the resources available within the group, which will suggest whether aims are feasible and attainable. Thus, in the interviews, the groupworkers communicate their purpose for the group, the objectives and structure they are proposing, and what may happen. Prospective members have an opportunity to outline their objectives should they join and to explore their reservations before deciding whether or not to commit. These feelings may take the form of expecting that membership will prove stigmatising, depressing or threatening to established ways of coping, or that it will prove ineffective in achieving change. It may be necessary to meet more than once before both groupworkers and members have a shared basis on which to make a decision.

Where social workers plan to join a preexisting group, at this stage they offer themselves to the group. This involves communicating what they believe the group can aim for and achieve, how this might be done and how they might be able to assist. Role negotiation begins here. Again, it is useful to compile a personal profile. Preparatory discussions are an opportunity for members to outline how they view the group and its tasks, and for groupworkers to assess whether they feel they can facilitate the group's tasks and process effectively.

On the basis of this exploration and negotiation, those involved can assess whether their original formulation, their overall aim and main target for intervention need to be adapted, after which they can formulate specific goals and a programme for the group. The guiding principle is to be realistic and not over-ambitious. At this stage, with individuals and/or the group, a preliminary or interim contract can be agreed. A preliminary contract is used to cover the earliest stages of the work while issues and problems continue to be explored. An interim contract is useful when issues might be relatively clear and a commitment to work together exists but when full understanding or agreement has yet to be achieved (Preston-Shoot, 1989). These working agreements may be either mutual or reciprocal. 'Mutual' refers to those occasions when there is complete agreement on the issues to be addressed and the means by which this will be done. 'Reciprocal' covers situations where the goals of the parties may differ but where there is sufficient common ground that they feel able to commit themselves to working towards achieving each other's goals. Contracts should be kept as simple as possible, with targets that are realistic and language that is clear and understood. Groupworkers should be upfront about power, specifying the circumstances where legal duties or positional authority might be invoked. Each member should have a copy, a baseline against which to measure developments and outcomes.

At this stage the working agreement should include:

● Why people have come together in a group.
● Basic rules.
● Details about structure and purpose.

- Statements of initial objectives, expectations and responsibilities of members and leaders/facilitators.
- Objectives or specific targets which together comprise the group's purpose, subdivided into indicators that will point to the extent to which the objectives are being achieved.
- Dates for reviewing the group's progress.

Whatever is negotiated and planned at this stage will have to be reexamined once the group has begun since expectations of the group and the reality may differ, and since it is only in the first meetings that the extent of a consensus about the group will emerge clearly. The actual experience of the group may require alterations to be made. Put another way, the line between selling, working in, and ending a group is not necessarily straight – relationships and needs develop between members and between members and workers. Trust and communication will evolve and an interaction between personal and social goals will emerge (Manor, 1988). Contracts need to be sufficiently flexible to reflect such developments in the group, hence the importance of reviews.

5 | Planning group operation

Introduction

Once groupworkers and members have agreed to work together, they can consider how the group will operate: how long sessions should last, how long the group should run for, how sessions should be recorded and possible methods and leadership/facilitation styles. These questions are easier to answer when groupworkers and members have clear and agreed aims, and a view of the resources that everyone will be bringing to the group.

Setting

Location is important. Is it accessible physically and psychologically for members or do transport links, the building's construction and its other uses exclude or further stigmatise? Breton (1991) suggests that meeting on their turf may be important to engage marginalised populations, while Mistry (1989) concludes that location should be chosen to link members with resources in their own neighbourhoods. With preexisting or natural groups, their own locations should be used where possible.

Duration and frequency

Weekly meetings dominate the groupwork scene. However, is this the most effective pattern? For instance, greater cohesion may evolve from more frequent meetings (Schneewind, 1996). Some support groups may not need to meet weekly and less frequent meetings may be indicated where members are to be encouraged to complete tasks between sessions. In other groups, where the issues or problems that form the target for intervention are long-standing, complex or serious, more frequent meetings may be indicated. In fixing the group's length, groupworkers must balance their own resources with those that members bring to the group, and consider the group's tasks in order to ensure the most successful outcome. Arguably, greater weight is often given to the constraints on group-workers, such as the length of student placements, other work commitments, and the duration for which they feel that they can sustain commitment to a group, than to a structure related to group development or anticipated to be reasonable for an adequate completion of the group's task. Organisational interests, such as throughput of work, and the increasing adoption of off-the-shelf packages (Caddick, 1991) with their rigid configurations of sessions and timings, may increasingly be squeezing out consideration of differences in how people learn, the pace at which they work, and the complexities of people's needs and of group process. Other influences might include previous experience or a fear that long-term groups encourage dependency.

If duration is not given any thought, or is based on preconceptions and organisational pressures, or is fixed arbitrarily, there is an increased likelihood that the determined duration may prove inadequate for task completion and it may be impossible to extend the group's length. Time limits may mean that it is unrealistic to expect changes from groupwork alone. Groupworkers, with members where possible, should attempt some calculation of the length of time a group might require to establish trust, engage in its tasks and achieve its aims. In brief groups, goals must be limited, focus maintained, and interventions prompt, with high worker activity to facilitate interaction between members (Sunderland, 1997/98). When working with marginalised populations (Breton, 1991) time must be allowed for consciousness-raising and for mobilisation and organisation for social action. One alternative, then, is an open-ended group or one where length is considered frequently, with ending related to progress within the group. Duration should be determined by the purposes of the group and members' needs and resources. For example, where members already know each other or have formed already into a group, the time needed for trust to develop and for members to engage will be shorter than if the group is formed of strangers who will need to build trust before the work of the group can begin. This is not to suggest that short-term groups are inadvisable. Indeed, they can be useful for specific tasks such as focusing on transitions in members' lives or where the group-workers want to learn more about a particular issue or difficulty as it affects and is experienced by members prior to devising a longer-term groupwork provision. However, any time fixed should allow for both progression and regression since a group's development is rarely straightforward. Groves and Schondel (1997/98), working with survivors of sexual abuse, offered three twelve-week groupwork 'sets' so that members could develop the necessary intimacy and trust for sharing painful stories gradually. It should also allow for consolidation of achievements. Push too soon (Bensted *et al.*, 1994) and any gains made may be lost when people return to their personal and social environments that may have remained unaltered. Finally, it should allow for members to engage and negotiate group stages, otherwise termination might arrive at a point where the group is beginning to address its tasks.

The same degree of thought should be given to the length of meetings. Many groups seem to meet for one-and-a-half or two hours. Rather, groupworkers might follow the timing adopted by natural groups and, with groups they have formed, determine the length of sessions according to the group's aims and members' resources, for instance concentration spans and the need to settle and engage. The time allowed should be based on that required to enable the work to be completed, coupled with practical points such as the availability of rooms and the leader's own constraints. There is also the question of whether sessions should be of fixed length. This has the disadvantage of possibly cutting through interaction inopportunely. However, the advantages are security of boundaries for members and the ability to plan time after the group. A time limit helps to prevent drift (Doel and Sawdon, 1999b) but groupworkers should be attuned to contributions in the closing minutes of a group. Particularly in therapeutic groups, this is when members might offer personal concerns about which they feel hesitant, knowing that there is little time left during which they might be under the spotlight. This decision should be based on what is likely to promote the group's work.

One other question arises here, namely, how is the time available to be structured? Is the session to be subdivided, a technique especially useful in children's groups where their concentration on one task is limited? Again, the structure should be determined by the resources that members bring to the group and the objectives being pursued.

Contact between sessions

It is not uncommon for members to contact groupworkers between sessions but how are these contacts to be handled? Are they to be accepted or refused? Will co-workers respond jointly or not? Will these contacts be recorded and reported back to the group? Will the member be asked to raise their issues in the group? This is a difficult issue. Groupworkers may wish to appear helpful but feel they must ask the member to raise their points in the group; the member may then feel rejected, fuelling anxiety and making engaging with him or her more difficult. However, to respond may negate previous work done in the group or place the leaders/facilitators in the position of not working with the group as a whole. Groupworkers need to decide for themselves and with the group their response to such requests. From the outset it should be clear whether or in what circumstances the groupworkers will respond.

It is useful to consider the meaning behind contact. The member may have found the group experience distressing or confusing. They may have felt threatened within the group or have formed a strong dislike of some members and be considering leaving. Generally, it is likely that the member feels a loser in the group. Consequently, a number of questions occur. Why has this contact occurred now and how is it related to events in the group? What is the relationship between this member, the group and other contexts?

Contact should not be refused. Rather, the member should be encouraged to take responsibility for raising their issues in the group. The member may be re-experiencing difficulties in group situations or finding their significant others unsupportive of what they are trying to do. In this example, they can be invited to share these difficulties in the group, using other members for support. If the member's difficulties have a circular causation, that is, the problem is located by the group within one member but is, in fact, a problem in terms of how the group functions as a system, it may be appropriate for the groupworkers to name how the group is functioning and to challenge belief and action systems in the group without taking sides. This might be done, for instance, by asking who else might have the difficulties that this member experiences or how other members perceive that this member experiences them or the group. Retaining neutrality is important, that is, not being sucked into alliances where members can say that the workers are on their side alone.

Recording

Concern to make records more effective, and to establish recording as integral to good social work practice, has a long history, yet recording remains a residual activity (Preston-Shoot, 2003b). However, its importance cannot be overstated since recording helps to focus work, to monitor practice and to support effective partnerships (DH, 2000a). Recording enables groupworkers to give an account of their practice and to codify their assessments and professional judgements. They must be able, therefore, to compile, present and share records and reports when managing and being accountable for their practice (TOPSS, 2002). This key role has four components, namely:

1. To maintain accurate, complete, accessible and up-to-date records, including consideration of whether needs are being met, change promoted and disadvantage countered.
2. To provide evidence for decisions and judgements, having checked the accuracy of information with others involved and having considered different possible interpretations.
3. To implement legal and policy frameworks concerning access to records.
4. To share records with service users.

Government guidance (DH, 2000b) on compiling and maintaining records, pursuant on the Data Protection Act 1998, also stresses that records must be adequate, relevant, accurate and up to date. Good recording practice is located around three principles – partnership in compiling records, openness when information is exchanged between agencies, and accuracy between differentiating fact and opinion. Records must also meet standards now required by the integration of the European Convention on Human Rights into United Kingdom law by the Human Rights Act 1998. Article 3, the right to live free of inhuman and degrading treatment, article 6, the right to fairness in decision-making, and article 8, the right to privacy and family life, all impact on groupwork practice.

Thus, groupwork records have several main functions: first, to describe and understand what has occurred in each session and the group overall; second, to provide data for assessment, decision-making and evaluation; third, to note significant events as a basis for discussion between the workers, and between them and members, for planning future sessions and for discussion in supervision; finally, to identify by what means the work involving both individual members and the group was agreed, why and with whom.

The first task is to negotiate what records the agency expects and the extent to which managers and caseworkers may have access to them. The principle of confidentiality is central to social (care) work practice but members may expect and want information concerning them in the group to be shared with their caseworkers. Equally, a higher-order principle of child and/or adult protection, or crime prevention, may require that information be shared within and between agencies. Consequently, any decision on whether and how records are to be used outside the group should be made with group members and caseworkers.

The second task is to agree on the style to be adopted and on the purposes to which the records will be put. Thus (Hodge, 1985):

● Are detailed records of each group meeting to be kept?
● Who will write the records and what is to be recorded?
● To what use will the records be put and where will they be kept?
● Who may have access to the records?
● What needs to be recorded for the leaders/facilitators to work effectively?

In the spirit of partnership, individual and group records should be routinely open to members and, to counterbalance the groupworkers' perceptions, partly written by them. Different perspectives about problem definition and required services or interventions are not uncommon (Mayer and Timms, 1970; Preston-Shoot, 2003c). Hence, triangulation of data sources and data collectors can enable exploration of consensus and disagreement, and generate more reliable conclusions. What is recorded and the techniques used will depend on the group's purposes and how the records are to be used. If the records are needed for evaluating the group, the detail required suggests that the records should be more than verbatim reports of sessions. Whatever leaders and members record, it should be done immediately after the meeting when the group is still uppermost in their minds and what is recorded can be discussed in the group at the beginning of the following session.

The following techniques, in all of which members can participate, may be helpful:

1. Attendance registers: one description of a group. If problems of attendance are noticed, what action should be taken?
2. Sociograms: a visual diagram of, for example, strong and conflictual relationships in a group, of who talks to whom and who talks to the group. Sociograms are a useful tool for evaluation. For instance, where the aim is to improve members' peer-group relationships, diagrams from several sessions will reveal the extent to which their patterns of communication and interaction are changing or constant. Sociograms are circles with the names of members placed around the circles. Arrows to the centre indicate communication to the whole group. Arrows to individual members indicate a communication to that member. Different colours or types of arrowed lines indicate the nature of the communication.
3. Rating scales: useful for summarising who makes what types of contributions, who shows particular behaviours and how these develop within the group. Members can rate themselves. Ratings can be made of individual members, the categories depending on the group's purposes. Where the group aims to influence behaviour, ratings may be made of aggression with peers, withdrawn behaviour, acting out or cooperative behaviour, and constructive relationships with peers and facilitators. Where the group aims to monitor roles that members adopt in the group, ratings may be made of the extent to which individual members engage in task-oriented and/or process-oriented behaviours, such as keeping the group on task or encouraging others. Where the aim is to improve parent–child relationships, ratings may be made of the extent to which their interaction includes sharing of feelings, clinginess, listening, play and ease of separation.

Ratings can be made of the group, the categories depending on the group's aims. The categories should be defined clearly on a scale from one (low, minimal) to five (high). The findings may suggest areas on which groupworkers should concentrate. Scales can be designed to measure the extent to which:

- There is cohesiveness in the group.
- Members are supportive of each other, cooperative or competitive.
- Members exercise control.
- Members participate in the group, for example in determining the group's activities.
- Members focus on the group's task.

4. Sentence completion: useful after each session or at intervals and at the close of the group for feedback from members and for evaluation. Thus:

- The worst thing about the group is . . .
- The best thing about the group is . . .
- When I come to the group I feel . . .
- The most helpful thing about the group is . . .
- What I enjoyed about the session(s) was . . .
- What I disliked about the sessions was . . .
- What I found most difficult was . . .
- What I found easiest was . . .

Sentence completion can help members define goals for themselves or evaluate the impact of the group experience on their lives outside the group and define further work as a result. Thus:

- Next week in the group I would like to . . .
- I have been able to use what I've got from the group by . . .
- It has been difficult for me to keep this up when . . .

5. Audio and video recording: helpful for recording key developments in the group's life, for example negotiating a contract or obtaining feedback at the midpoint or end of the group. Members' permission should be obtained and an explanation given of how the tapes will be used.

6. Monitoring and measuring activities: in a group that aims to help members achieve a particular skill, recording methods that involve measures of the amount or quality of a particular activity may be helpful. For example, a chart may be used to monitor the length of time a child spends on one activity.

7. Standardised instruments: these are validated measures of, for instance, general health, dependency covering mobility, self-

care and domestic activities, strengths and difficulties, and emotional/behavioural disturbance. They provide information on the difficulties that members face from different people's perspectives. Repeat measures can catalogue groupwork's impact.

8. Reports: what is included in reports of each session and the overall group will be influenced by who the report is for and what groupworkers and members feel is relevant to their work in the group. What follows is a list of possible headings:

- Themes within the session
- Each member's contributions and behaviour. Are changes noticeable?
- Which members were leaders, which followers? Who was scapegoated or isolated and why?
- Relationships between members and between groupworkers and members
- Have subgroups or pairings formed? What is their effect on the group?
- The climate of the group
- Agreements and decisions reached: what and how?
- Ideas given by group members
- How the group developed. Did it work well? Was everyone involved? How far have the group's goals been achieved? How fast is it progressing? What is impeding or facilitating progress?
- What changes have been made to the group's purposes? Why?
- What roles did the groupworkers adopt (giving direction, exercising control, stimulating or suggesting, advocacy outside the group)?
- How did the co-workers interact?
- What are the groupworkers feelings about the group?
- What is the plan for the next session or for future groupwork services?

Where reports are written after every session, periodic summaries helpfully clarify progress and suggest areas on which groupworkers and members need to focus.

Methods

Various methods are available to groupworkers, from discussion to more experientially based activities. Action methods may assist groups to move closer to difficult themes or topics (Doel and Sawdon, 1999b). Groupworkers may have some notion of suitable methods prior to meeting members. This may be based on models, skills and knowledge with which they are familiar, for instance systemic therapy or encounter groups, or be influenced by the type of group they envisage. Certainly the methods used must suit the leaders but they must suit the members too, be selected in consultation with them and be appropriate for the group's aims, stage of development and work. Choice of methods should relate to the needs and capabilities of members who must understand the rationale for their use. That is, chosen methods should have a specific purpose, help the group achieve its aims and be within the ability of members to use (Douglas, 2000).

Methods are not mutually exclusive but can be combined. Whatever methods are used, ground rules should be established that address any special needs amongst members and respect their right not to participate (Lordan, 1996). Standardised packages are increasingly in vogue, for example with sex offenders. Drawing often on approaches evidenced from research, they may be quite effective (Bensted *et al.*, 1994; Hayden *et al.*, 1999). They may additionally offer security to groupworkers (Brown, 1996) but only if they endorse the principles on which such programmes are based, for members will discern any groupworker discomfort with the packages and quite possibly disengage. Equally, if not used flexibly and creatively, and if not matched to people's learning styles, these programmes and the methods they contain may not be tailored to the needs of individuals or groups. Their use may become mechanical, whereby groupworkers focus on what comes next rather than what is emerging through the process and dynamics of the group as developmental opportunities. Thus, Blacklock (2003) cautions that groupworkers should be wary of following over-rigidly off-the-peg programmes without doing work to underpin or consolidate the exercises they contain.

Games can be used to create a therapeutic, trusting environment and to focus on group or personal development, through emphasising communication, imagination, trust, confidence-building, self-disclosure and relaxation. They encourage members to share perceptions of themselves and each other, feeling cards being one method of enabling members to communicate how they perceive or are affected by others. Games, such as the waiting game and rounds, can be used for control, feedback and generating ideas. Indeed, the use of structured activities can facilitate bonding and identification, promote awareness of internalised oppression and commonality, and enable sharing within a safe distance (Groves and Schondel, 1997/98). Thus, Hayden and colleagues (1999) used a feeling–thought–action sequence through exercises as a learning method. The exercises generated responses about day-to-day experiences through which members could reflect on and learn about their behaviour and emotions associated with offending.

Role play and drama give members an experience of what it is like to be someone else and can be used, for example, in groups concentrating on developing social skills, to practise behaviours or to dramatise problems or difficulties experienced by members. These experiences can open up discussion and, when accompanied by use of video, can also reinforce learning. They are a useful technique for providing members with understanding of their behaviour, their relationships, feelings and attitudes towards others, and how others react to them.

Movement can be used to develop skills in expressing emotions and in non-verbal communication, and to improve relationships between members. For example, dance and movement can be used to improve the bonding between parents and young children. A group may engage in work tasks, such as the organisation of petitions, both to achieve social change goals and to foster individual development. Finally, groups may use discussion, either centred on topics introduced by members or groupworkers, or free-floating, perhaps picking up group themes. Groupworkers may find that the group works quicker and is less anxiety-provoking if they highlight topics where this is compatible with the group's aims. If co-workers have different ideas about methods, this can disrupt the environment that they are seeking to create to foster the group's work and result in one of them becoming uninvolved.

Sculpting is a useful tool for demonstrating the emotional positions that members put each other in, a physical portrayal of how one member sees people's positions and attitudes towards each other. It is a moving picture that facilitates exploration of the possibility of change in a stuck situation (Hayden *et al.*, 1999). First, a current situation or set of interpersonal relationships is moulded. Then, people are moved into the desired situation, noting what needs to happen to achieve this transformation. In a group sculpting may enhance the perceptions of conflicts in a group. It may build up members' skills by sculpting their perception of the group so that they can see how it feels to be fixed in a position into which they place others. It may enhance a group's supportive potential by building up care skills through members' perception of relationships within the group. Sculpting enables members to be aware of feelings about one another which, otherwise, they might be unable to acknowledge or verbalise. It can break through barriers of verbal communication and language, stimulating thought and creativity and taking learning to a deeper level of understanding (Lordan, 1996). It can elicit impressions of the group's structure and may free and focus communication, making explicit implicit relationships, roles, mutual perceptions and expectations. It provides information on the group's structure and behaviour, which may stimulate discussion on changes that would facilitate the group's functioning. Alternatively, it is a tool for identifying, experiencing and discussing interactive processes between this group and others (Lordan, 1996).

Frequently groups generate metaphors through their discussion and/or activity, for example of mining potential or being on a journey of change. Metaphors can be used to help people reframe their thinking, and to address issues by finding new alternatives through which to perceive them. They may assist in the development of cohesion and closeness if they can be generalised to incorporate the differences that will also exist in a group (Sunderland, 1997/98; Hayden *et al.*, 1999). Alternatively, films and books, if used carefully (Weinstein, 1994), can open out such issues as racism and sexism, and offer moving insights about processes and dynamics that might facilitate the group's work. Similarly, the use of photographs can be a medium through which people can communicate their personal biographies, their experiences and feelings, and/or the nature of the environments in which they live.

Circular questioning is another method that addresses the phenomenon of perspective, namely that what a person sees, believes and experiences depends on where they are positioned in systems (Stratton *et al.*, 1990). Circular questioning involves avoiding blaming and attributions of madness or badness, and maintaining neutrality, that is, not siding with one against another but rather questioning everything. Information is collected about views of the problem, the group's beliefs and organisation, by encouraging members to verbalise what they believe other members and people outside the group would say. Circular questioning explores differences, particularly changes in relationships around significant events, and elicits ratings and rankings of behaviour, feelings and interactions by asking one person to comment on a dyadic relationship in the group or on what another member might say about them or the group. It aims to perceive differences and change, for example before and after an event, on the basis that differences are information.

Leadership styles and roles

Another preliminary before the first session is to consider what style of leadership or facilitation to use and what roles to adopt. Groupworkers may already possess expertise in particular areas or have clear style preferences which may lead them to determine the roles they will adopt beforehand. However, to develop fixed ideas about roles too early, perhaps out of a need for security, is inadvisable since the plan may be inappropriate or fail to take account of members' needs and resources or the evolution of the group. Styles and roles must be appropriate to the group situation, the outcome wanted and members' capabilities (Douglas, 2000). Thus, as a newly formed group develops and members acquire confidence in their skills, groupworkers may relinquish central responsibility for determining the focus for each session.

One distinction to be clarified is that between leadership and facilitation. Grindley (1994) envisages facilitation as providing a process to enable the group to discuss its own content. The facilitator is concerned with process and good communication, being neutral about content and having no stake in decisions. By contrast, an animator seeks to help people discover and use their potential, share their concerns, set goals and plan action. An animator helps people to think creatively and critically when identifying problems and finding solutions. This role appears similar to Douglas's (2000) conception of facilitating leadership where groupworkers demonstrate that control and use of a group's resources are available to members, who can develop power and skill in their deployment. For Mullender and Ward (1991) the refusal of a facilitator to be directive can be frustrating but necessary if members are to assume responsibility. However, facilitation does not equate to non-intervention. A facilitator will resist any passive acceptance or dependence that members may bring and will challenge members about what they are proposing to do and how. Facilitation, then, is akin to systemic therapists who adopt positions of curiosity (enquiry and challenge) and neutrality (refusal to take sides) (Stratton et al., 1990).

Another distinction is between leadership functions or roles and leadership styles.

---

putting into practice: observing styles

Three groups discuss the lived experience of social (care) work. Two observers, whose task is to capture group dynamics and processes for subsequent discussion, watch each group. Each group leader is given a style to adopt – authoritarian, democratic, laissez-faire.

An authoritarian or directive approach may feel safer (Douglas, 2000). The group may appear productive as tasks are demonstrated, directed and carried out. However, everything revolves around the leader and group process can become insensitive, even coercive, or show evidence of dependence, apathy, submission, overlooked contributions, withdrawal, hostility and competitiveness. Similarly, a particularly charismatic leader may appear empowering and generate excitement but ultimately relationships within and surrounding the group may remain unchanged (Weinstein, 1994). Outcomes may not endure because they are dependent on the leader's energy.

A democratic or partnership style works for consensus and inclusion, and the development of positive, supportive relationships. The group may initially appear unproductive but, as motivation, participation and satisfaction increase, it may demonstrate a high level of creativity, cooperation and output. A laissez-faire style, where the leader hardly participates in task discussion or group process, may engender frustration, even aggression, as time is spent discussing options and as the group lacks coordination. Poor outcomes and withdrawals are likely.

However, the situational nature of leadership means that the style adopted must suit the group's needs at that moment. For example, a more directive style may be appropriate with a newly formed group where people are unsure what is expected of them, or in a group where quick decisions are required in a crisis or where routine business is being conducted.

One typology for the exercise of leadership offers four roles, namely:

1. Emotional stimulation – using challenge and modelling, risk-taking and self-disclosure.
2. Caring – providing support, acceptance, praise and security, where leadership is concerned with the engagement, cohesion and trust required for purposeful work.
3. Meaning attribution – using clarification, interpretation and acknowledgement of feelings to understand people's experiences and to develop individual and group resources; working on how to translate these group processes into people's lives outside the group.
4. Executive function – concerned with the framework for the group, as in setting limits and goals, rules and pace.

It is generally assumed that the higher the caring and meaning attribution, the greater the likelihood of positive outcomes. Too much or too little emotional stimulation and executive function, the less likely is a positive outcome.

Another typology of possible roles (Dowling, 1979) includes:

● Introducing tasks, opening and concluding sessions.
● Proposing – putting forward new concepts or suggestions.
● Building – extending or developing the actions, proposals, comments or contributions of oneself or others.
● Supporting – agreeing with others.
● Disagreeing – declaring a difference of opinion or criticising others.
● Openness – disclosing personal experiences or feelings.
● Testing understanding and consensus – what is the group mood?

- Integrating – summarising and clarifying the discussion or content.
- Eliciting – seeking information, opinions or clarification.
- Giving information and opinion.
- Bringing in – involving others.
- Challenging a behaviour or comment to provoke expression of feelings or perspectives.
- Enlarging – expanding the meaning of contributions by interpreting or providing awareness of connections or underlying dimensions.
- Pointing out – highlighting another's behaviour or contribution that has not been recognised.
- Encouraging and maintaining the group task.
- Observation of the group's process.
- Harmonising – bringing about compromise.
- Discouraging or reinforcing behaviour.
- Verbalising the group's concerns.

It is not just formally designated leaders who can exercise leadership (Doel and Sawdon, 1999b). Experts by experience can also offer direction – structuring the task, guiding group process, providing resources, building non-hierarchical relationships and evaluating progress (Braye and Preston-Shoot, 2005). This can be demonstrated by thinking through an approach to 'what if' scenarios. There are not necessarily right answers here but anticipating potential situations may enable groupworkers and members to draw on previous experience, to explore the contribution of theory, and to be accountable for their practice.

---

putting into practice: what if?

How would you approach such group situations as ...

➤ Someone leaves the room?
➤ Some members decline to join in activities?
➤ Some members want to change an already agreed programme?
➤ Someone dominates or is disruptive?
➤ Someone says that they do not want to attend any more?

Factors external to the group

Groups do not exist in isolation from their environment. Indeed, many founder because their base is not established securely within wider systems. Thus, it is as important that groupworkers concentrate on the environment in which they are practising as it is to focus on the group's structure and operation. Indeed, environmental factors can undermine a well-planned group.

Significant others

The cooperation of significant others outside the group is important. Just as for effective groupwork the leaders/facilitators will be helped by a cooperative stance from their colleagues and agency, so too for members. Their aims and membership may be frustrated by hostility, indifference or incomprehension within their families and extended networks. Therefore, it is useful to consider what the attitudes of significant others will be to members joining the group and whether some work needs to be directed at these systems prior to and during the group. This could include explaining the group's purpose, stressing the importance of regular attendance and the undesirability of parents using non-attendance as a punishment for children.

Thus, Doel and Sawdon (1999b) recommend including significant others in the initial offer of group membership. Lebacq and Shah (1989) held preparatory meetings with parents and discussed ambivalent feelings about the group, confidentiality, managing the child's behaviour and coping with questions. They also held support meetings during the group and undertook a post-group evaluation. Breton (1991) refers to consciousness-raising about the socio-economic features of problems amongst not just group members but also their communities. Hopmeyer and Werk (1993), working with bereavement groups, recognised that members might have to return to an empty environment. This is one example of how the scope for change may be affected by what surrounds the group. Douglas (2000) therefore advocates assessing the possible responses and effects of the environment on the group and the adoption of a strategy to maximise the beneficial effects and to minimise the negative impacts.

Agency considerations

Groupworkers have found that they must be prepared to work for change in their own agencies if they are to engage successfully with marginalised populations (Breton, 1991). They must anticipate concerns (Kolbo *et al.*, 1997/98) as well as mobilise groupwork values and knowledge. Heap (1992) reports how unsystematic and ineffective in influencing priorities and change and in sustaining groupwork in their own agencies groupworkers had been. Put another way, colleague, line management and stakeholder ownership and support are vital to success (Hayden *et al.*, 1999; Doel and Sawdon, 1999b, 2001).

Senior (1991) describes how ambivalence and narrow agency goals within probation services' management curbed creative practice, particularly when it emphasised empowerment and social action, and how a criminal justice system preoccupied with risk and offences focused on set tasks and missed developmental opportunities with clients. Similarly, Mistry (1989) reports the problems faced by women workers in acquiring funding and establishing groupwork as credible in a climate that considered specific facilities for women as marginal to mainstream probation practice.

Groupworkers may also find colleagues unhelpful, ambivalent or defensive because they see groupwork as a threat to established ways of working. Since many practitioners (prefer to) work with individuals and families, they may be unconvinced of groupwork's value. Many supervisors are inexperienced in supervising groupwork. This absence of support can weaken groupworkers' confidence and motivation, or increase their isolation and anxiety. Groupwork may take place too in a climate of limited budgets where groupworkers have to compete for resources and convince colleagues of the need for and viability of a group. Consequently, Brown (1997) suggests conducting a feasibility study within the agency, exploring the resources, staffing and management support available for the group's objectives. A secondary contract with the agencies involved may also be advisable once the group commences to ensure that promised support materialises.

In such an environment groupworkers will have to draw on several spaces (Preston-Shoot, 2003a) to challenge resistance within policy development and service design, to seek a secure base for their work and to encourage managers to examine more critically the outcomes or effectiveness of the practice within their own agencies.

The knowledge space

Groupworkers might refer to different knowledge bases to advance alternative ways of understanding and tackling the issues that confront the agency, and to demonstrate groupwork's usefulness through a clearly articulated theoretical and practice rationale. They can utilise narratives from experts by experience, the research evidence, practice wisdom, the parameters created by legal rules and ethical principles, and stakeholder evaluation of needs and outcomes.

The practice space

It is good practice to present proposals to colleagues, to invite comment and to discuss the resources needed for the group and the implications of this for the agency's overall commitments. It might be helpful to identify the agency's functions, acknowledge its constraints, and promote interventions in a way that enables the agency to perceive that its service objectives are being met (Preston-Shoot, 1992). Groupworkers should be aware of whom they should consult and inform, what authority they have in the group delegated by the agency, and how the group might contribute to the overall service being offered by the agency. Thus:

● How is the group to be explained to members, their families and the clients who are not included?
● What liaison is necessary with those who have referred or might refer people to the group and what feedback will be given to them?
● To whom are the leaders/facilitators accountable and for what?
● Whose authority and support is required? Who are the key people to engage?
● Who needs to be informed and consulted?

The group space

Groupworkers might discuss the agency's attitudes with group members and examine whether the group has a task in engaging with the agency in a dialogue about its attitudes and the services it provides.

6 | Preparing to facilitate or lead groups

Introduction

In their research Doel and Sawdon (2001) found that workers rated as important participation in training and time for reading and reflection. Preparation is essential for effective groupwork. This chapter will outline how this may be done and provide frameworks through which groupworkers can develop their confidence and skills. Preparation is necessary each time practitioners engage in groupwork. Every new experience will involve familiar and unchartered challenges and will trigger expected or unanticipated preoccupations and concerns. To some degree every group will initially evoke reappraisal of and uncertainty in skills and expertise once confidently taken for granted. As Douglas (2000) observes, groupworkers need to grow into each group as their skills and understanding will not automatically carry over.

Being groupworkers requires practitioners to be able to tolerate a degree of separateness from the group in order to fulfil their roles. Doel and Sawdon (1999b) refer to facing apartness, recognising that whatever their similarities and differences with members, their role is separate from the group. Moreover, practitioners may mistrust groups, concerned about their potential for destructiveness or about encountering unmanageable resistance. They may fear losing control of the group or of having to deal with members' hostility, disappointment or dependency, or of being sucked into situations in which they become enmeshed. Groupworkers may respond to these pressures by adopting a directive, controlling, authoritarian approach. Alternatively, they may seek to reduce the expression of emotions in the group or to remain unexposed, reflected either in withdrawal from members or in an overemphasis on listening and non-directiveness. Again, they may emphasise their expertise and their interventions may appear to be intellectual and 'textbook' rather than related to members' communications and group needs.

They may feel the pressure to be liked, emphasising what they share in common with group members and stressing the importance of friendliness, tolerance and positive feelings. If these pressures are not to paralyse groupworkers and distort communication and perceptions of the group (Williams, 1966), or lead them to abdicate leadership, careful preparation is essential.

Practitioners need to anticipate what a group may arouse in them and whether they feel able to participate in the tasks of the group. This involves them considering their fears, feelings and expectations of the group and whether they can make a contribution in the group from the knowledge and skills they possess. They will also take earlier experiences into this group and they will need to have the ability to control or contain personal needs and problems if they are to engage successfully with members. They will need to identify their skills and their relevance for the group's tasks. They will need to be flexible in their use of groupwork models if they are to ensure that the needs and problems of the group are met effectively as they emerge.

Co-leadership

Doel and Sawdon (2001) note the relative success of co-led as against solo-led groups. The choice of co-working groups may be inspired by reluctance to facilitate groups alone. This may be because groupwork training on qualifying programmes has been minimal (Marsh and Triseliotis, 1996) and practitioners lack confidence in the relevance of their experience, knowledge and skills. It may be because groupwork is not an accepted and established method of working within an agency and practitioners have to work hard to gain acceptance of the modality and to cope with discouraging events.

However, where one worker is coping well already, co-working is contraindicated. It is similarly inappropriate where practitioners hold divergent goals, styles and expertise since this can create uncertainty, miscommunication or lack of clarity in the group and will make it difficult for the groupworkers to work well together. In groups where the aim is to encourage members to express their views to organisations, or where the purpose is to enable them to assume responsibility for group direction, structure and programme, one worker may be the most appropriate. Otherwise members may feel outnumbered, threatened or intimidated by the presence of co-leaders. Two workers may prove too top-heavy in a small group but may be useful with activity groups for monitoring and control. Using three or more workers can create both confusion regarding the structure of and roles in leadership and a situation where leaders and members form and coexist as subgroups.

Co-leadership does provide continuity for the group when one leader is absent. However, the absence of one leader can prove just as disruptive as no session at all. Groupworkers will have to judge how important continuity will be for a group and, where important, how best to maintain it. Where it is anticipated that there may be problems containing or managing members' behaviour, or involving members in the group's tasks, co-working may be indicated provided that the groupworkers have an agreed strategy and feel that the group is likely to consider two leaders more seriously than one. However, a single groupworker may be able to formulate effective strategies for preventing or responding to difficulties such as hostility, and co-working may neither prevent nor make it easier to deal with problems of disruption or dependent behaviour. This is because members may react negatively to what they perceive as an excessive presence of power and authority in the group (Whitaker, 2001). Co-workers may feel more comfortable when encouraging or managing the expression of powerful emotions, and be able to push each other to avoid comfortable sessions where there is empathy and support but no impact or challenge. Similarly, they can respond to demands from individuals or subgroups for attention without loss of direction elsewhere in the group.

Co-working may be chosen because of the advantages it is seen to convey for groups and for groupworkers (Preston-Shoot, 1986). Where the aims and purposes of a group include work in subgroups, co-workers can link each subgroup's work in order to move the whole group forward. Co-working can provide members with an opportunity to experience the interest, concern, involvement and authority of different people. For example, Hopmeyer and Werk (1993) describe a professional/peer-led model where co-leadership was valued because the peer facilitator offered a role model and the professional groupworker kept track of task and process.

---

putting into practice: solo or co-working

> Will groupworkers find it easier to facilitate the group towards its aims alone or with a colleague? Would one worker, for example, feel overwhelmed or find controlling and containing the group difficult?

> What are the possible benefits and outcomes for members and groupworkers if solo or co-leadership is adopted? Will there be tasks and processes to manage and monitor such that co-workers could cope more effectively with the volume and complexity of the group's material? Is more than one view about what is happening in the group or evaluation of group dynamics important?

> Will members find it easier to use the group for the set purposes if there is one leader? Where, for example, the centrality of the workers for the group is to be de-emphasised, will leaders emerge more easily from within the group if there is only one leader?

> What skills are necessary for the practitioners to possess for this group and would one leader have the resources required? Where, for example, it is intended to feedback observations about significant events and dynamics, would this be easier with a co-worker?

Co-working can model effective interactions, offering a cooperative and creative relationship based on collaboration, trust, clear communication, constructive use of difference and the expression and resolution of disagreements (Groves and Schondel, 1997/98; Blacklock, 2003). For example, advantages accrue for members from seeing a black–white partnership take equal responsibility and challenge racist attitudes and behaviours (Lebacq and Shah, 1989; Mistry and Brown, 1991). Where co-workers are of opposite gender, this can provide the group with a valuable experience of a partnership working collaboratively with mutual respect without destructive competition, exploitation or pervasive sexuality (Yalom, 1995). The model provides the group with the opportunity to reassess stereotypes and to make overt disagreements within it, to work through feelings about authority figures, and to experience discomfort without permanent harm.

Where there is an emphasis on task accomplishment and monitoring, observation and commentary on group process, responsibility can be shared between co-workers. One can engage with group process while the other 'holds' it (Lordan, 1996). Co-workers can share or accept total responsibility for monitoring the group's process, that is, individual and group behaviour, and recording events as they occur, or for initiating tasks with the group and attending to individual member's needs, feelings and behaviour (Hodge, 1985). Choices here may depend on practitioners' different strengths. Equally, co-working offers two perspectives through which to analyse situations (Blacklock, 2003), both how to understand and respond to group dynamics and how best to facilitate the group's work, enriching the resources available with which to keep focus and respond to a group's many events and needs (Hodge, 1985).

For groupworkers, co-leadership offers a training opportunity for less experienced practitioners (Hodge, 1985), an opening for continuing professional development through a relationship with a colleague (Yalom, 1995), as well as a source of support and feedback generally. To maximise this benefit, practitioners should be enabled through supervision to identify and evaluate the impact of groupworking on their skills and resources and to consider whether these are adequate for the task. This may be facilitated with questions like:

● What personal goals am I setting for myself?
● What am I hoping to learn through co-working?
● What skills and resources do I want to develop?
● What have I learned and what is the evidence for this?

Co-workers can clarify each other's contributions and challenge or compensate for any feelings that each may have of limited skills and competence. The support may encourage groupworkers to be more adventurous in the group, having a colleague to indicate whether an intervention is appropriate. Sharing responsibility may help workers when they feel stuck, uncertain or lost (Whitaker, 2001).

Ultimately, the nature of the group, rather than its size or composition alone, and the resources that groupworkers bring to the task should determine whether co-leadership is appropriate. The appropriateness of a co-work partnership should be kept under review as planning proceeds, and details of group membership and purposes and the resources of individual groupworkers become clearer. Planning with a co-worker preferably should begin before either has given much detailed consideration to the group. The further planning has reached prior to the introduction of a co-worker, the more difficult it might be for one worker to relinquish control of the work and for the newcomer to feel that the project is a shared endeavour in which they are able to contribute and develop their ideas and skills. This is true especially for leaders who join a group because a previous groupworker has left. In this circumstance the groupworkers should first establish a sound relationship and then review the group's aims. This is to ensure that the contribution of the incoming groupworker can be accommodated and that differences of opinion concerning aims, methods or goals will not interfere with the group's functioning. Conflict is possible unless the newcomer is given time in preparation to discuss their thoughts and feelings about the group and allowed to influence previously made decisions (Hodge, 1985).

Selecting a co-worker

It is possible to define those factors that contribute to a sound partnership and enable a group to work effectively.

Shared values and theoretical orientation

Mistry and Brown (1991) pinpoint shared values and congruence on theory, Reynolds and Shackman (1994) to having a core agreement, for instance on how to handle differences. A belief in groupwork as a method of intervention is required both to sustain their involvement with a group and to engage the agency in the project. This is a commitment to 'thinking groups' as well as identifying the grounds for justifying groupwork as a modality of choice. Preparatory work will be necessary to ensure that co-workers share values and similar basic assumptions, for example about contributors to mental distress or offending. This involves co-workers testing out their beliefs about the nature and causes of members' problems and the compatibility of their groupwork practice principles and theoretical orientation. It involves identifying the influences on their thinking about groupwork and their theoretical approach (say, psychodynamic, systemic or eclectic) and preferred ways of working. This is not to suggest that co-leaders should share identical interests, beliefs or values, but that their views on group aims, how these are to be achieved and how they will facilitate the group should be sufficiently compatible for them to work effectively together (Hodge, 1985).

Shared group aims

Whitaker (2001) stresses the importance of compatible stances, by which she means co-workers sharing similar views about their approach to the group, what they hope the group can accomplish and how they will function in it. Compatible attitudes are necessary towards the variety of problems and situations that may emerge in the group. A clash of perspectives and a failure to examine inevitable points of conflict or develop a consensus on aims and procedures for a group will result in the group and its leaders having difficulty understanding its development and taking forward its work. Therefore, at the outset, co-workers should establish whether they hold similar views about how to facilitate the group and the techniques and skills required for this. Ideas about the group, what the work is about, and on aims and expectations need to be broadly similar. Both leaders and members need to believe that the theoretical propositions underpinning the group and the related practical methods to be used are coherent and likely to be beneficial (Hodge, 1985).

Professional skills

Since co-work and groupwork are demanding personally and professionally, co-workers must feel confident with each other. Otherwise, it may prove difficult to exploit the advantages that co-work offers, particularly in terms of modelling, and the co-workers may be more vulnerable to splitting by the group's members. Several qualities appear significant here. First, an ability to keep to group aims and to challenge and work without feeling threatened within the partnership. Second, a belief that colleagues can manage the group experience confidently and competently. Third, a willingness to identify what strengths they offer and where they are relying on a colleague's skills.

Not uncommon is the fear of not being good enough or a self-assessment of limited confidence. Co-working is likely to be a rewarding experience where colleagues are comfortable to be with and engender feelings of self-worth and respect for each other's skills. Helpful too is willingness to engage in developing the strengths and resources they already have, and to participate in confronting knowledge and skill gaps.

Attitudes to co-work

Co-workers should be prepared to devote time to developing the partnership. Every co-work partnership will experience stress and encounter differences, will be susceptible to conflict, and will be tested by groups (Hodge, 1985). They should be willing to exchange constructive feedback and have open and honest attitudes towards resolving conflict and tensions, working at the group's aims, and discussing divergent views when preparing for and working with the group. They should be prepared to disclose their thoughts and feelings related to problems or circumstances addressed by the group so as not to offer members or each other misleading signals based on separate understandings concerning what the issues or problems are about (Hodge, 1985). They should feel able to communicate clearly and resolve problems without experiencing negative repercussions from each other. Otherwise they may become distant from each other, lose awareness of how group processes are influencing them, and signal to group members that expressing disagreements and differences harms relationships (Hodge, 1985). They may inappropriately assign difficulties to their co-worker rather than locate them within the group or the wider systems impacting upon it. They may discourage members from exploring what is happening in the group.

Style

Compatible but complementary styles are important (Mistry and Brown, 1991). They offer a greater degree of diversity and potential richness for the group, and enable practitioners to concentrate on those skills and methods congruent with their style, freeing them from the feeling of having to be competent in all the tasks required. Similar styles and strengths can result in omissions and in avoidance of particular issues both within the partnership and the group.

For example, if both practitioners work at similar levels of intensity, this may make their detachment from the group process difficult. Where the co-workers are over-united, members may have difficulty in making an impact on them. Equally, having too divergent qualities can create difficulties in communication and leading the group coherently. The most effective partnership is one where there is differentiation, where the partners combine different strengths within a shared stance and values relating to the group (Whitaker, 2001). Therefore, groupworkers should understand their partner's style of work and preparation should include focusing on how workers practise in groups and their possible contribution to this group.

Gender combinations

Loosley and Mullender (2003) suggest that where group identity is important, co-workers should be of the same gender; where issues and concerns are to be addressed, an opposite-sex combination might enable stereotypes to be challenged. A male/female team may provide a balanced, effective model and opportunity for the group to work through misconceptions and fantasies concerning the co-workers' relationship. It provides members with the possibility of experiencing a functional relationship. A mixed-sex partnership may be indicated when working with a membership comprising partners and examining relationship difficulties.

Professional status

Mistry and Brown (1991) highlight the importance of thinking through issues surrounding different levels of experience and conveying to the group how co-workers will work together. Where different levels of experience exist, less experienced groupworkers may have little self-confidence and be concerned about how they will be perceived. The more experienced groupworker may feel that the relationship lacks balance and that too great an onus rests upon them. Both may collude with an uneven distribution of tasks, with the result that little learning or professional development occurs for either. Group members may become aware of differences in skills and authority, and relate or respond more to the experienced groupworker.

Similar dynamics may occur when one groupworker holds a more senior position in the agency, where the partner and members may invest them with greater authority, even if they are the less experienced groupworker. Where the co-workers are drawn from different professions, perceptions of professional status may influence how much authority they are accorded. Even where co-workers hold similar agency positions, the change in context and the need to redefine roles and relationships should be recognised. Otherwise potential problematic role–relationship issues in the agency could be taken into co-working in the group. Consequently, a clear understanding of roles and authority for this group is necessary (Hodge, 1985).

Presenting co-work to the group

Frequently the question of explaining the presence of co-workers in a group is neglected. However, Mistry and Brown (1991) suggest that explanation is essential to counteract stereotypical roles and assumptions that authority and power rest with one, for example white and/or male, practitioner. Members may be puzzled by or suspicious or uncertain about the use of two facilitators. They may react by showing preference for one worker based on a perception of status or on roles adopted by the groupworkers in the group. They may attempt to undermine the relationship, especially if they feel intimidated. If the co-workers do not discuss these dynamics, they may find themselves competing for or colluding with members' attention, thereby diverting energy away from the group's tasks. Equally, failing to provide an explanation contradicts the commitment to partnership with experts by experience. A simple and truthful explanation at the outset is good practice, for example that two workers offer different perceptions, experience and skills for the group and can ensure that the many events in a group are not missed.

Preparing to work together

Successful co-workers combine a shared ethos about groups and the aims for the group in question with dissimilarity in terms of skills and strengths brought to the group. Some differences in personality are also desirable, for example between directive/

interventionist and passive/observer, but not so extreme that one worker's contribution smothers the other's. The emphasis is on complementarity and differentiation, which should provide a healthy model of interaction and functioning for the group and help to dispel myths that differences are unhelpful.

A creative relationship, based on trust and collaboration, does not emerge immediately. Time is needed for co-workers to understand each other's thoughts and feelings about groupwork and their ways of handling situations in a group, and to develop an inner security in relation to the group so that neither will be unduly dependent on the other for support in the face of group pressures (Hodge, 1985). Time is required to allow trust to develop, sufficient for co-workers to feel secure enough to critically evaluate their working together and to challenge each other.

Lebacq and Shah (1989), preparing for work with black and white sexually abused children, discussed childhood and culture, their experiences as women, and the differential effects of racism on them. Mistry and Brown (1991) explored power and control and how racism and sexism might interplay in their co-working. They based their decision to work together on an assessment of compatibility, especially congruence on theory, values and practice principles, their ability to deal with conflict, risk-taking in self-disclosure, and their ability to work on the race dimension in their partnership and subsequent groupwork. Mistry (1989), looking further at mixed-race partnerships, again stresses the importance of co-workers being responsive in considering their own history. Focusing on sexism, Blacklock (2003) argues for the need to take care when allocating work so as not to perpetuate gender myths, isolate the female worker or collude with a male worker joining only with male group members.

Reynolds and Shackman (1994) warn against relying on unspoken assumptions of what partnership is. They gave careful attention to defining their roles in the group and to familiarisation with each other's approaches. Using some of the exercises which follow, they recognised how the creativity of a partnership depended on their ability to confront imbalances in their relationship, to overcome fear of disagreement and failures to communicate expectations and intentions, and to share their reactions to the group's subject matter. Before and during their groupwork, they recognised how leaving to the other areas where they felt less confident limited their contribution and learning. Consequently they took time to learn from each other's style and to share their ideas.

Nosko and Breton (1997/98) also comment on the need to avoid becoming frozen in a particular position and to develop congruence in their combined efforts so that co-workers' concerns do not take precedence over those of group members. Hodge (1985) stresses the importance of exploring whether differences in practice orientations or group-related beliefs are sufficiently significant to suggest that difficulties might occur in working together. The tools that follow are designed to assist groupworkers to explore the potential of a co-work partnership, and to develop support and mutual understanding. They offer a means of recognising, using and maximising groupworkers' strengths and skills, of exploring working styles, and of sharing knowledge about responses to group processes and situations. They enable workers to share and work through anxieties about working together, such as competitiveness or feelings that the partner will be the more effective groupworker.

---

putting into practice: personal profile

➤ What is my social work and groupwork background – training, experience of group membership and leadership?

➤ What have been my previous experiences of co-working?

➤ What have I learned from these experiences?

➤ What values, theoretical orientation and styles of groupwork do I bring (Hodge, 1985)?

➤ What do colleagues and service users say are my encouraging patterns in how I work?

➤ What are my likes and dislikes about groups and groupwork?

➤ What makes me feel uncomfortable in groups and how do I respond to tension and conflict, to members I find it hard to relate to, and to particular types of group problems?

➤ What are my strengths and weaknesses when facilitating groups?

➤ What are my expectations of a co-worker and what are my personal learning needs?

➤ What learning opportunities do I feel able to offer to a colleague?

➤ What do I see as the advantages and disadvantages of groupwork?

➤ What expectations do I have about being a groupworker?

Practitioners can write out and then share their ideal co-work relationship. They may hope to learn from a co-worker and to find creative ways of working. They may expect co-work to be a source of support and feedback whereby they may gain in confidence as groupworkers. The same may be done with their more fearful fantasies, for instance that their weaknesses will be exposed in the group. Co-workers may be anxious about whether they can form a good working relationship or about sharing responsibility and control, despite wanting to do so. The rationale for this exercise is that practitioners will bring to each new encounter fantasies, expectations and assumptions based on prior experiences. If these are not to form the basis of subsequent dissatisfactions and disappointments, they must be acknowledged openly and worked through. This may help to diffuse anxieties and to ensure that present practice is not impeded unduly by past events.

---

putting into practice: sentence completion

What do I need to know about my co-worker to help me understand their thinking?

> ➤ I agreed to consider working with this group because . . .
> ➤ My expectations, hopes and fears of working with this group and this co-worker are . . .
> ➤ Things I would prefer my co-worker not to know about me are . . .
> ➤ Things I think my co-worker should know about me (style, orientation, experiences, feelings about groups, theoretical influences) are . . .
> ➤ The skills I have as a groupworker are . . .
> ➤ The groupwork skills I want to develop are . . .
> ➤ What I want to contribute to the work includes . . .
> ➤ What I hope my co-worker will contribute includes . . .
> ➤ The skills I feel my co-worker possesses are . . .
> ➤ The characteristics of my co-worker that cause me difficulty are . . .
> ➤ What my co-worker may find difficult about me includes . . .
> ➤ Things I have wanted to ask my co-worker are . . .
> ➤ Things I imagine about my co-worker include . . .
> ➤ Things I see in my partner (outwardly visible characteristics) include . . .

Questions of working style, preferences for task-oriented or group-maintenance roles, assuming or relinquishing leadership functions, and exploring the effectiveness of communication can also be explored through the use of exercises. These will show who prefers leading and initiating, who prefers to respond, and the co-workers' ability to accept and relinquish leadership. Subsequent discussion can highlight preferred styles of working and evaluate the degree to which co-workers feel comfortable with each other. Issues of communication and trust will surface. Learning from the exercises and subsequent discussion can be used to evaluate how far a particular partnership is appropriate for a group.

---

putting into practice: fantasy house

Holding a pen together and without speaking, co-workers draw their dream house. This may be followed by discussing what happened, how they experienced the exercise, and whether and how conflict was resolved. (Donnellan, 1981)

---

putting into practice: describing a shape

Sitting back to back, one co-worker designs a shape and must then instruct the partner to draw that shape without using gestures, turning around or telling them what the overall shape is. Each partner should have the opportunity to communicate and receive. The workers can discuss how they experienced the exercise. (Donnellan, 1981)

---

putting into practice: mirrors

One co-worker is nominated as leader and their partner must mirror everything the leader does. Roles may be reversed and the exercise concluded with neither partner being the nominated leader and with each choosing whether to mirror the actions of the other or to initiate an action of their own. (Donnellan, 1981)

Conclusion

Preparation influences outcome. That said, it is a misconception to suppose that no further consideration of leadership and co-work is necessary once some initial preparation has been completed. Each co-work relationship is a dynamic entity that will hopefully develop over time. Similarly, a groupworker's skills, knowledge and confidence will hopefully also develop through stages which, while not necessarily unidirectional, should indicate progression providing consultation is available. At the outset groupworkers may be preoccupied to some degree with anticipation and apprehension, enthusiasm and nervousness. They may question their competence to respond to group issues as they emerge and they may feel the need for information and security. Co-workers will have to become accustomed to each other in the group, such that at times they may operate more as two individuals than one partnership. Self-consciousness characterises this beginning.

As groupworkers experience their co-worker's styles, strengths and limitations, they will increasingly be able to utilise each other's skills and compensate for each other's difficulties. More of a viable joint enterprise will develop, as should confidence for taking forward task and process work with the group. There should follow a stage of trust where co-workers feel confident, can seek and value suggestions, and can learn from and anticipate each other's actions. Taking forward task and process work with the group may not always feel smooth but activity will feel more purposeful, with the workers more interdependent, drawing on each other. With sufficient time, groupworkers will feel much more in control of their work, integrating new understanding and skills into their repertoire, and feeling comfortable with self-criticism and appraisal from colleagues. The availability of supervision will help groupworkers to develop an understanding of the dynamics of the co-work relationship, of the group, and of their ways of working.

7 | Working with groups

Introduction

When groups work well, they can be highly productive. This chapter will concentrate, therefore, on how groupworkers can facilitate the transition from a collection of individuals towards a common purpose and sense of cohesion where members feel valued for their contribution and enabled to engage in the group's tasks. It will focus too on how practitioners may understand events in groups, such as silence or the expression of hostility. Finally, the chapter will trace how groupworkers may gauge a productive balance between task and process, being central and more peripheral and, when co-working, between individuality and integration in response to group dynamics and their own increasing confidence in their roles and skills.

The first meeting

Right beginnings are vital. How a group begins will influence members' attitudes towards it and each other. How groupworkers initially interact with a group will influence the degree to which they are afforded credibility (Lizzio and Wilson, 2001). Joining a group is not easy. Members may find the idea of a group strange despite having discussed its formation, aims and possible benefits with groupworkers and others. They may be suspicious about its purpose and the groupworkers' roles, especially if their membership is involuntary. They may experience heightened anxiety from uncertainty about what to expect and the nature of demands made of them, how they will be perceived or whether the group will help them. They may fear rejection, either exaggerating their difficulties to demonstrate their need for help or minimising these to gain respect. Whether or not membership is compulsory and the group formed or pre-dating groupworkers' involvement with it, members may come with a positive attitude towards it or with ambivalence, defensiveness and aggression. If these feelings remain unacknowledged they can impede members engaging in the group experience, prove traumatic and disturbing, or foster insecurity and anger. Thus, Doel and Sawdon (1999b) advise groupworkers to anticipate members' likely thoughts and feelings in order to 'tune in'. Groupworkers interrogating their own feelings may also provide clues. Lizzio and Wilson (2001) advise groupworkers to engage with participant concerns and to deal with issues, assumptions or expectations affecting their engagement, using, for instance, questions or sentence completion (Preston-Shoot, 1989) that invite discussion of members' experiences, hopes and anxieties about groups and this group.

The needs with which members come, and which they may or may not expect the group to meet, might already be openly stated and shared by virtue of their presence, such as when joining a group established to improve parenting skills or assist people to cope with bereavement. Alternatively, some needs might be stated but the depth or understanding of them more private, such as addressing drug use, or needs may be hidden from oneself or from others, such as feelings of inadequacy. Groupworkers, therefore, will know more about groups than about members' lives (Douglas, 2000), at least initially. Opening out lines of communication, enabling members to assess the degree to which they can work with others and facilitating working relationships (Lizzio and Wilson, 2001) can be assisted by questions that address how people come to be present.

From earlier interactions people will come together with some information regarding the group's structure, purpose and aims. However, groupworkers should not assume that goals or the nature of the group are clear. Members may, for instance, express their needs differently in the group from previously. They may feel now that they have had little choice but to attend. One task then is to develop a common perception of and investment in the tasks or, as Lizzio and Wilson (2001) write, to ensure that individual and collective outcomes are clear and agreed, and procedures established through which the group will aspire towards them.

A structure for a first meeting might run as follows. First, general introductions, their nature dependent on group purpose and type. Building a team might start with each member offering three insights into their names. Research groups might open with members describing their involvement with or interest in the topic (Braye and Preston-Shoot, 2005). Members can give their reasons for coming or, where group purpose is negotiable, identify what issues concern them (Preston-Shoot, 1989).

Second, groupworkers provide some information about themselves, especially their relevant experience and their motivations behind this group. Sometimes this may involve elements of self-disclosure. Whenever groupworkers disclose information about themselves, this should promote the group's purposes and not be motivated by personal needs. If the group is to make a difference for members, and if they are to participate actively, groupworkers must outline the opportunities presented by it. The task of raising motivation and confidence is helped by groupworkers making their intentions and resources specific, being clear about why they are there and not defining aims so broadly that they are limitless, for instance to increase self-confidence. Groupworkers should also present their own values and encourage discussion of how value principles, such as challenging oppressive behaviour, will be managed (Preston-Shoot, 1992). This helps members to assess whether they can work with the groupworkers and to establish initial relationships (Lizzio and Wilson, 2001). Positive outcomes are associated with workers establishing an approach recognised as legitimate by members (Hayden *et al.*, 1999), and building trust through clear communication of purpose and of confidence in groupwork as an effective way of addressing issues (Bensted *et al.*, 1994).

Third, discuss with members how problems will be tackled in the group. How norms are set so that the group can take responsibility for its functioning is an early choice point depending on group type (Hodge, 1985). Douglas (2000) proposes that setting ground rules early can accelerate focus on group tasks, although their implications may not be fully understood and their acceptance may be at a rational rather than a feeling level. Papell (1999) argues that groupworkers laying down rules immediately treats a group mechanically rather than as a human experience. Understanding and acceptance of rules is a group's process. Thus, in one group (Braye and Preston-Shoot, 2005), groupworkers invited members to articulate behavioural norms and subsequently to review at each meeting the approach to be taken by all to control group process – codes of conduct for working together, confidentiality, and 'what if?' scenarios.

Fourth, it may be appropriate for groupworkers to discuss authority with the group. Working from empowerment and partnership principles requires an open discussion of power and the nature of accountability owed by groupworkers to employers, regulatory bodies, the group and themselves (Preston-Shoot, 1992), space for members to express feelings derived from their experiences, and a clear explanation of negotiable and non-negotiable positions. There may be situations where groupworkers would want to stress their positional authority, arising from their agency mandate or from their role as group leaders. They may wish to stress their sapiential authority, the knowledge they bring to the group. They may choose to emphasise members' sapiential authority – the knowledge and expertise they bring, which recognises that members can be leaders or facilitators of the group also (Douglas, 2000). Convening focus groups for research purposes would be one such example. However, members may view the groupworkers' authority differently from the workers themselves. For example, groupworkers may wish to be seen as models or to encourage group rather than leader-directed discussions. Members, however, may see them as powerful representatives of an agency or as figures who possess information and expertise or the power to authorise or prohibit behaviour. These perceptions will affect how members see the groupworkers and interact in the group. If differences in perception remain unacknowledged, group aims may remain divergent.

Fifth, discuss the group's purpose and structure. Members are more likely to remain in a group if it begins from where they are, if they feel that they can obtain satisfaction from membership, and if their apprehensions are openly acknowledged. This, and the development of cohesion and consensus, is helped where the group's task is clear, where aims and purposes are negotiated and where specific objectives are formulated within the overall aims. Useful pointers here include:

- What are members' expectations and why are they present? Distinguish between motivation and persuasion since the latter can be demotivating.
- What might they be asked to do?
- How do members explain their problems or circumstances?
- Explain why members were chosen and establish boundaries, such as when and if new members will be admitted.
- What can the groupworkers offer the group?

- Anticipate possible reactions, attitudes, resistance and areas of commonality. Connect members. Acknowledge feelings and encourage their expression, especially relating to membership. Are there any stumbling blocks to engagement?
- Locate and discuss any problems between members and between them and the groupworkers.
- What content? How might the goals be achieved? How negotiable is the programme? Who sets the agenda? The advantages of members deciding the agenda are that the group begins where the members are and it encourages them to contribute their own resources. The drawbacks are that it can mean a slower beginning and raise members' anxiety. One way forward is joint planning.

The more relevant and realistic the aims, the better groupworkers will be able to give members a clear basis for joining, proposing suggestions about aims and methods, making contributions and evaluating progress. The degree to which groups work with individual and group needs and objectives will vary. A social action group, working for external change, or a research-inspired focus group will concentrate less on individual needs, the working agreement essentially being with the group. In contrast, a therapy group may emphasise both individual and group objectives, such that contracts will be negotiated for the group and individual members. Member and groupworker goals do not have to be identical but, where differences emerge, assessment should conclude whether it is possible to work together. An interim agreement enables people to work together for a period followed by review. A reciprocal contract accepts that groupworkers and members have different aims but envisages cooperation to help them achieve their divergent goals (Preston-Shoot, 1989).

Members' goals may also diverge. Here the group must resolve how much difference it can tolerate within a collective agreement about its purposes and structure. Thus, the process of contracting involves member–member and member–groupworker interactions, focusing on task and goals but also procedure and structure: what kind of group this is, what types of contributions are sought, how the group will do things and how people will treat each other. Making and reviewing contracts, which can be written or verbal, centre then on group process, interpersonal exchange and tasks.

Agreements must be sufficiently flexible to accommodate group development, hence the importance of reviews, and should cover:

● Framework – confidentiality, boundaries, norms, attendance, frequency, recording, reviews, resources.
● Substance – what inspired the group, desired outcomes, methods, tasks and responsibilities, and how progress will be assessed. (Preston-Shoot, 1989)

This structure may take more than one session to complete, it may be revisited, and it should not be rushed because this attention to contracting does seem to enhance members' commitment and to facilitate group process and outcome. The groupworkers' task is to promote the group's existence as a group, an objective that may require that they summarise what needs to be dealt with, acknowledge different views, involve quieter members and point out areas of commonality. Lizzio and Wilson (2001) describe the groupwork task here as 'process architecture'. Groupworkers' tasks include enhancing choice about whether and how people participate, establishing members' presence in the group, constructing a working environment and building productive relationships, clarifying outcomes and processes and enabling the use of knowledge and skills related to purpose.

Work within and between sessions

The structure and programme for sessions should be clear and correspond to expected group dynamics, issues and tasks. How and on what the group works should be recognised by members as promoting collective learning and, therefore, individual and social action (Breton, 1991). The programme should be sufficiently flexible to respond to external pressures that encroach upon members' lives (Mistry, 1989). Predesigned groupwork packs may prove insufficiently responsive to member needs. A programme that is not feasible within the time available may provoke disappointment and disengagement, as may one that underestimates members' capabilities and expertise.

Preceding meetings form the context for succeeding meetings so groupworkers should not overlook or underestimate what is carried forward (Malekoff, 1999). This is one aspect of pre-session preparation, tuning in again (Fatout, 1997/98) by reflecting on group history, significant events and problems in past sessions, group stages and dynamics, and the relationship between the group's environment and its goals and content. There is a clear relationship between a group's effectiveness and the time given to review-informed planning. Depending on the nature of the group, review can encompass what works within the group, what alliances may be developing and their impact on the group's task and member development, and how the group's resources are developing and being used. Review can scan emerging and preoccupying themes, particular problems or processes within the group that might need to be managed, and whether goals and methods remain appropriate. Finally, review involves further consideration of roles and tasks, and of how the group can consolidate what has been achieved.

In self-help and self-directed groups, groupworkers are not leaders and should avoid uninvited interventions since the group is responsible for content and process. Rather, their roles are those of initiators (of resources and support), facilitators (of organisation for task and process) and consultants (making knowledge available) (Habermann, 1990; Matzat, 1993). Facilitation includes helping the group to analyse the causes of particular problems and then to set its own agenda, priorities and task allocation, identifying power issues in group process and enabling members to address conflict and difficult issues (Mullender and Ward, 1991). Co-workers model and promote non-exploitative relationships, information exchange and partnership working, facilitating members to extend their focus when planning and to review and reformulate as appropriate, especially having checked for exclusion based on discrimination.

Working from empowerment and partnership principles also requires groupworkers to beware taking charge too easily (Preston-Shoot, 1992; Nosko and Breton, 1997/98). Groupworkers may be invited to assume levels of responsibility and control that are dis-empowering – to be an expert, to comment on an interesting issue. Groupworkers may become anxious because of the different pace and time frames with which people approach the challenge of learning and change. Partnership and empowerment practice requires developing a shared sense of purpose by:

● Maximising involvement in problem definition, paying particular attention to how members interpret their situation and creating opportunities for them to acquire knowledge and skills in order to increase their understanding and their power to take action.

- Offering space to negotiate and take decisions jointly.
- Consulting about language to develop shared understanding about terminology and to ease communication.
- Thinking systemically – looking wider than the immediate situation.
- Challenging assumptions, stereotypes and behaviour, which reduce the authority of a member's voice, within and outwith the group.
- Using the spaces that values, legislation and knowledge provide for individual and social change.
- Encouraging broader redefinition of issues, linking the personal with the structural.
- Acknowledging people's strengths, encouraging collective action and connecting members with other sources of power.

---

putting into practice: power and partnership

> When in groupwork do you feel powerful and where does this power come from?

> When in groupwork do you feel powerless and why?

> How does your power affect those you work with in groups? How does your power empower or disempower others?

> What power do group members have and how easily can they exercise it?

> How can you increase their sense of power? How can you empower them?

> What power and authority do you need to work effectively in this group?

> What do you feel about giving up power and control? What effect would this have on your work?

Working from partnership principles means hearing and not reacting defensively to members' anger towards professionals for how they have intervened in their lives (Hill, 2001; Braye and Preston-Shoot, 2005). Equally, when holding dual roles of groupworker and statutory agent, making authority accountable means more than being open to feedback (Bodinham and Weinstein, 1991; Preston-Shoot, 1992). Groupworkers can be clear about when and how they will use their legal mandates, how personal issues might be connected to wider issues that the group can seek to tackle, and what other networks are available with which individuals and the group can usefully connect. To hope that the need to exercise statutory authority will not arise may ultimately prove more disruptive to group process than to acknowledge the possibility, to recognise members' anxieties about it and to establish principles for its use.

In early group meetings, and perhaps throughout, exploring internalised oppression may prove necessary. This can be promoted through the use of storytelling and/or using reframing to identify the positives in what someone has achieved, followed by an expression of curiosity about what may be limiting how individuals or groups respond to a situation. Verbally or pictorially (say by sculpting or describing a river denoting significant events and their impact), groups can explore how context affects behaviour and people's resilience and resourcefulness. Groups offer an ideal setting for challenging how beliefs and behaviours constrain new ways of thinking and acting because they reduce individual isolation, offer role models, and provide time and a setting where feelings can be recognised and validated, encounters simulated, decisions supported and achievements praised. Then, by providing advocacy, protection, connection and 'holding', as appropriate, groups can help members resist a return to previous powerlessness. Members may acquire confidence from enhanced understanding of their situation, making successful choices and gaining control over their problems.

However, groups must respect an individual's need for defences and effective work requires a sense of trust and safety (Turkie, 1992). Reflection rather than direct challenge may be more effective in getting beyond barriers. Here, as elsewhere, patience is a key groupwork skill. If group members have developed trust in each other and the groupworkers, and a sense of safety, skilled facilitation will enable them to question themselves and others, understanding will grow and changed behaviour and perceptions will be achieved.

Throughout, co-workers should focus together on how to share or divide out the practical and emotional task and maintenance work. Without role clarity their interventions will be muddled and uncertain, confusing and counterproductive. Co-workers should feel able to intervene, whatever prior decisions have been agreed about role responsibility, and should experience their contributions as valued. Accordingly (Hodge, 1985), who will assume responsibility for task issues (achieving goals, giving and seeking information, initiating and summarising)? Who will address themselves to process interactions within the group and the emotional atmosphere of the group (observing and evaluating the climate, building trust, resolving conflicts, verbalising themes)? Who will focus on issues within the group and who on events outside it but affecting its dynamics? How will meetings be opened and closed? How do the groupworkers propose to engage members? How will difficulties in the group be handled?

Where co-workers have different levels of experience, roles may be divided initially on the basis of the more experienced worker being more central. However, the confidence of the less experienced worker may increase and after several sessions they may feel able to take a more active role. It is useful, therefore, to review regularly the needs and development of the co-workers, perhaps in supervision, and to revise role relationships when indicated.

They should also reflect on the impact of this work on them. Their own felt readiness for the group may contain important information either about the co-work arrangement and/or the material in the group, on which supervision discussions, and debriefing after each session (Hill, 2001), can focus. Groupworkers should acknowledge their own 'baggage' that is unrelated to the group, such as the influence of their personal lives on their functioning. They should consider any unresolved matters between the co-workers, since these can be stirred up by the group experience, and what tensions they may have taken out of the group. For instance, unexpressed concerns around compatibility of styles, the degree to which practitioners prefer to be directive and central, use self-disclosure, or comment on processes and themes, can create negative consequences in the group (Hodge, 1985). It may indicate the need to review their interaction, using such questions as:

● How well do they feel they worked together and supported each other?
● What have they appreciated and disliked when working together?

● In what areas do they feel improvements in their working relationship are needed and how might these be achieved?
● How have their hopes and fears about the partnership worked out in the group?
● Do they feel able to develop their own style and skills, and what knowledge and skills are they acquiring?
● Are roles initially adopted still appropriate? How are the roles working out?

Reviewing group interactions involves reflecting on what effect members have had on the groupworkers and vice versa. Group-workers need to identify their reactions to members and the issues they bring to the group, especially where these have some similarities with their own life situations or difficulties. Members may attempt to split the groupworkers, perhaps because they feel ambivalent or resentful about membership and/or detect imbalance or tension between the groupworkers (Hodge, 1985). Similarly, co-workers can sometimes mirror in their relationship the group's behaviour. They may become competitive, wanting to be the best liked, the most insightful. They may adopt roles of expert or authority figure, or overemphasise listening, withdrawal and over-identification with members as a defence, a security operation in response to group material or doubts about their groupwork skills. They may feel depressed or angry, feelings transferred from members and which can be mistaken as their own feelings. The group may leave them feeling inadequate and not in control (Hodge, 1985). Reflection here is about making sense of what they are experiencing in order not to act out these feelings in the group.

Stages in groups

Groups develop and change. The duration of any stage is related more to the group's history, context and dynamics, and to the groupworkers' skills, than to time, although in short-term groups the latter stages may not be reached or tasks and processes within them fully worked through. Stages are not necessarily sequential or unidirectional. A group may be at different stages for different tasks. Members may also proceed at different speeds, reflective of different attitudes towards personal development and change (Henry, 1988; Douglas, 2000).

The value of conceptualising group stages lies in enabling group-workers to tune into group process and respond appropriately. It lessens, for instance, the likelihood of asking a group to do something for which it is insufficiently integrated (Douglas, 2000). For open groups (Henry, 1988) it suggests that new members can be more effectively introduced when existing members have negotiated storming or conflict passages and that groupworkers might find ways of recording the group's journey and marking stages in its development as a means of consolidating its progress. The recognition of an initial orientation phase suggests that contracts are more appropriately formalised once members have concluded the joining stage.

However, the stages have been variously conceptualised, reflective of different types of group. Behroozi (1992), working with involuntary clients, gives five stages beginning with orientation where members may exhibit eagerness and ambivalence, hostility and suspicion. This is followed by dissatisfaction, which includes rivalry and curiosity, resolution, production and termination. Schiller (2003), using a relational model of group development, also gives five stages – pre-affiliation, establishing the relational base, mutuality and interpersonal empathy, which includes intimacy and differentiation, challenge and change, and separation/termination. She sees conflict as developing once mutuality and connection between members are present and then as equating more to constructive challenge than vying for power and control. This contrasts with Tuckman's model (1965), which positions storming after forming and before norming, performing and adjourning.

Common to all conceptualisations is the first, joining stage, characterised by separateness, difficulty in sharing and an absence of cohesion. Members, while hopeful of encountering shared experiences, may have reservations about the group's viability or membership, particularly when they know very little about the others and why they are there. Members will be anxious: are people like me? How do they react to me? Should I engage with this group? How much do I say or disclose? This stage is marked by members seeking similarities, shared interests and background, values and attitudes from which to develop commonality, norms and a definition of themselves in relation to the group's tasks and their role within these. A hierarchy and leader, often the most assertive member, may emerge. Members may seem dependent on the groupworkers, especially for approval and guidance, but this may be accompanied by suspicion of their intentions, anxiety about the group's tasks or testing out their understanding, reliability, authority and concern.

Groupworkers are central in this stage, having brought the group together or offered to assist an already formed group. They should aim to demonstrate that members have something to offer each other, that their resources are information for the group. They should decide the style of introduction with this in mind and guide the group in establishing communication and defining roles consistent with the group's goals. Their task is to emphasise the group's aims, functions and boundaries, to hold the structure open and to prevent domination by individual members. Their task is to open up issues rather than provide definitive answers, to instil confidence in interactions, to anticipate members' concerns about the group and to focus on members' hopes rather than perceived deficiencies. Concerning the group's emotional and maintenance needs, groupworkers should facilitate the search for commonality, helping members express and compare experiences and expectations, and locate common problems. Too passive an approach may undermine cohesion. Too authoritarian an approach may result in over-reliance on the groupworkers and underestimation of the group's resources. It may push the group too far or fail to begin where the members are.

With growing cohesion members will begin to work as a group, identify with it and develop clarity and consensus about its objectives. The group works towards an agenda of issues, begins to analyse why the problems or issues on the agenda exist, and establishes what action to take (Mullender and Ward, 1985). Members will begin to share and explore relationships within the group although this may take longer in open groups with changing membership (Schneewind, 1996). Initial roles become established, such as who offers what type of contributions, as members take personal decisions on the degree of intimacy and risk-taking to accept and work out the organisation or structure most appropriate to the group's task. Standards of behaviour and rules in order to accomplish tasks and maintain cohesion may be worked out (Hodge, 1985). There may be some dispute and testing out of roles, for instance over leadership of the group, but the emphasis is more on conformity than challenge in order to keep the experience 'good' and avoid confrontation. Members will begin to develop a sense of what is required but may still depend on approval and be uncertain about their performance in the group. Members may question the usefulness and aims of the group but identify with and commit themselves to it, establishing rules and norms. They may react with optimism on finding that other members share their concerns, or that groupworkers practise from partnership and empowerment principles, but also with anxiety when they realise that there is more to membership than just sharing issues. This stage is a process of finding a way to contribute to the group and of coping with being a member.

The groupworkers' role here is to help members use the group. This may involve opening up issues, involving all members, and clarifying what they will or will not do. It involves transferring responsibility gradually to members for the group, offering feedback and comments rather than controlling direction. It may involve checking their perceptions of the group with members or attempting to introduce flexibility into the group's structure. Concerning the group's emotional needs, groupworker tasks may include attempts to identify commonality, to promote safety, to demonstrate understanding and their availability as a resource, or to offer support and guidance. If members do express hopelessness, this may be because they doubt that the group will make a difference or have yet to find a means of approaching their tasks. By identifying resources within and outside the group and by providing guidance on how the group might approach its tasks, groupworkers may enable the group to progress. Again, too little or too much control and the group will not become cohesive and effective since both approaches reduce the learning opportunities available to members.

One stage often omitted from frameworks is that of revision. Groups may return here several times unless the original definition of aims proves sufficient. This phase involves questioning of original aims or of group norms, structure, duration or behaviour as they have evolved. Review presents opportunities to identify and consolidate areas of competence within the group besides clarifying purposes, evaluating what has been achieved and reanalysing the problems and issues being tackled. The group may reaffirm or modify methods and actions previously decided in response to its tasks. The more members are central to this phase rather than groupworkers, the more they may experience gaining control over their lives and decisions (Mullender and Ward, 1985). Schneewind (1996) suggests that self-help groups may experience such a phase where they redefine and reintegrate using their original purpose as a baseline or move to dissolution.

A well-functioning group is marked by clearer and purposive aims where the group's influence on members is high, cohesion is strong and structure stable. Members work flexibly and cooperatively on the group's tasks, with interaction marked by increasing experimentation, support, room to change, ability to be different and constructive challenge of each other. Leadership is diffused throughout the group. Groupworker tasks here revolve around pulling back from major responsibility for the group, emphasising how members provide support, direction and control by drawing on their experiences, skills, knowledge and strengths. Other tasks include maximising members' self-esteem, offering observations on preoccupying themes or task accomplishment, and reminding the group of its objectives if members are concentrating on its uniqueness for them.

Once a group develops its own life and identity it can be difficult to bring it to an end. Denial, expression of new or old needs and of feelings of loss, affection, anger or ambivalence and evaluation of achievements are reactions (Ross, 1991) that may be designed to avoid or to manage an ending. Groupworkers may struggle with closure but ending is more likely to be experienced as non-rejecting when groupworkers have:

● Been clear about ending from the beginning and have involved members in planning for it.
● Reviewed the time limit throughout the group by questioning whether it remains appropriate and counted down the sessions.
● Talked specifically about what members will miss and what they will take away from the group experience in terms of friendships, learning and achievements.
● Focused on how members will adjust to being without the group (Ross, 1991).
● Evaluated what the group has achieved, what progress has been made, and worked through to consolidate how members can use the outcomes of the group experience outside and after it (Bodinham and Weinstein, 1991; Ross, 1991).

● Used gifts, photographs, booklets and/or ending rituals.
● Reinforced the group's work through follow-up and identified whether gains have been sustained or further work is indicated.

A central task is to help members acknowledge feelings of sadness and loss, though these may be mixed with relief or feelings of increased autonomy and pride in achievements. Groupworkers need to be prepared for the expression of negative, rejecting or rejection-provoking behaviour. This should not be ignored or denied but equally groupworkers need to beware of being trapped by guilt into premature or inappropriate offers of further help. Therefore, the idea of review is critically important. The group may require more time to achieve its aims or consolidate progress. Where there has been some progress the group might continue if there appears to be the potential for further change and if clear aims can be formulated or if consolidation of work already achieved cannot take place without the groupworkers' intervention. Put another way, extension is desirable if ending is related to progress made, if only to prevent members becoming part of a revolving-door syndrome.

Equally important when thinking about termination is focusing on ending the co-work relationship – their feelings of loss of an interesting piece of work or a close partnership. The supervisor has a role here in helping groupworkers to evaluate their work and learning, to integrate this appraisal into their future practice, and to understand and manage their responses to the ending itself.

Understanding interactions

Many things happen in groups. Vernelle (1994) comments that some individuals pursue aims that interfere with the group's task, into which others may become drawn. Douglas (2000) suggests that individuals bring habitual responses to group encounters. These responses may trap them in vicious circles. Someone who feels unable to share their thoughts, feelings or needs may become seen as distant, self-sufficient or unreceptive, having little to offer; others may ignore this individual, reinforcing their wariness about self-expression. Someone who feels the need to be accepted may prioritise conformity rather than difference; resentment may build until negative feelings are expressed more strongly than is appropriate, which may reinforce conflict avoidance.

If individual dynamics can complicate interactions, so too can group process. For instance, an unproductive group may be the outcome of groupworkers being overprotective, providing support without challenge, or demanding too much of members whose dominant experience has been of marginalisation (Breton, 1991). The point is that behaviour conveys a message and meaning. Behaviour may concern difficulties an individual has in this or all groups. Anxiety about being heard might, for instance, lead to silence or domination of discussion. Alternatively, explanation for particular interactions may reside within the group. For example, groupworkers may be expecting the group to talk freely about personal issues and to respond to interpretations, when members do not feel safe to engage or lack the necessary verbal skills. Difficulty in or fear of talking with others may result in a group where feelings are suppressed, while a group characterised by constant unloading of feelings may reflect confusion about how to manage need (Turkie, 1992).

To understand interactions, as a prelude to action, groupworkers might look for patterns. What effect does group structure have on communication, individual member engagement and satisfaction, and the group's efficiency (Vernelle, 1994)? There are three levels when reflecting on communication patterns. Communication between pairs may be characterised by mutuality – similar or complementary exchange – or by dependency and dominance where the one controlled is not free to participate in the group. The relationship may be complementary, where differences blend together, or more destructive, where one individual provokes attack and where the group may be sucked into taking sides. Communication between triads can also be characterised by mutuality – interlocking contributions of similar quality – or by alliance, where two may gang up to attack another or find protection from this third person. Communication may take the form of mediation, where one tries to bridge difficulties within a pair, or competitiveness in which two individuals try to outbid each other for the attention of a third. Within the whole group, communication may be circular, where everyone participates in exchange. Alternatively, communication may revolve around a leader, generating less participation, or it may pass slowly up and down a chain. When there are subgroups, some members may be excluded from some communications.

Similarly, groupworkers can describe critical incidents and formulate ideas about why these occurred and what individuals and/or the group gained (Lumley and Marchant, 1989). The sequence 'what is the problem?', 'who is it a problem for?' and 'why is it a problem now?' may generate useful ideas about how to intervene (Stratton *et al.*, 1990).

Scapegoating

A scapegoat is a member who is isolated, attacked or accorded low status and onto whom the group projects feelings it finds unacceptable. Until these are addressed the group will maintain the situation, the process diverting energy from the group's tasks. The scapegoat will feel ostracised, unable to gain acceptance. They may withdraw, become aggressive or accept the role and attempt to gain approval by behaviour that attracts attention. For reasons connected with personal needs, they may find this negative attention satisfying.

The scapegoat position may arise by chance, for example when a newcomer is attacked because this does not disrupt group bonds. It may be a group response to one member whose behaviour or difference creates dislike or impatience within the group. Groupworkers may scapegoat a member who does not conform to their expectations.

Groupworkers too can be scapegoated, as happens to the jury foreman in the film *12 Angry Men*, perhaps because they communicate uncertainty about how to facilitate the group or ambivalence about exercising their authority. Groupworkers need to understand what kind and intensity of scapegoating are taking place since this will indicate what action is appropriate. Accordingly, why has the role emerged in the group? What, if anything, does the individual get out of the role? Direct intervention to protect the scapegoat or to challenge the group may be necessary. Groupworkers may comment on underlying issues or projections in the group and encourage members to examine their attitudes and to accept different or difficult behaviour. They may involve the scapegoat explicitly in some aspect of the group's work.

Silence

A quiet group can be disorientating. Groupworkers may feel inef-fectual. However, silence is not always threatening or symbolic of resistance, disinterest and aggression. It may reflect positive devel-opments. Therefore, groupworkers should tune into its meaning, into what is being communicated.

Silence may indicate that change has taken place and that members are thinking through a new situation in the group or a different understanding. Groupworkers may acknowledge the change and any disorientation felt, and encourage members to discuss their thoughts when ready to do so. Silence may reveal uncertainty about how to proceed, in which case groupworkers may summarise what has been achieved or suggest what perhaps concerns the group, and contribute ideas about tasks facing members and how these might be accomplished. Silence may reflect an absence of hope about effecting change, fed by members' social positions and experience of oppression and exclusion. Additionally, members may be uncertain about how to achieve their goals, unaware of resources in the group, and unclear about whether mutual understanding exists. Groupworkers may need to draw out what members have to offer and perhaps become active in sum-marising, guiding and linking what members say, and in identify-ing how the group might challenge perceived powerlessness.

Where silence indicates anxiety, insecurity or defensiveness, members may need encouragement to participate. Silence may feel to them good or bad, comfortable or uncomfortable (Lumley and Marchant, 1989). Groupworkers should demonstrate understand-ing and acceptance. If judged appropriate, they might hypothesise about emotions present in the group and/or recognise people's indi-vidual backgrounds. They might explicitly value an individual's experience before asking a direct question. They could use circular questioning, engaging less silent members in expressing views about an individual's silence before checking back with that individual on who has reached closest to their experience. If silence reflects oppo-sition, boredom, indifference or suspicion, groupworkers should model openness to criticism. It may be that they have misunder-stood the group's needs and readiness to address important issues, such that a review of the group's tasks is indicated.

Dominant members

Sometimes one or several members dominate the group and compete with one another or the facilitators. This domination can result in other members contributing little to the group. Equally, it can divert the focus away from the group's work. Groupworkers can positively connote points being made by one individual and then invite other group members into the discussion or activity before, perhaps, returning to invite the dominant member to summarise the discussion. The use of circular questioning may again prove effective:

● What does the dominant member think other members might say? Do they agree?
● How does the dominant member think others view their contribution in the group? Do they agree or disagree and in what respects?
● Who in the group most/least agrees with this member?

A degree of firmness may be necessary sometimes to redirect the discussion, to involve others, and to tactfully curtail a dominant member's contributions.

Groupworkers might also reflect on the meaning behind the attempted domination. It may represent a fear of close relationships or of not being heard. It may indicate anger about past experiences or be members' habitual approach to group membership and to seeking attention or care-giving. In some groups it may be appropriate to name possible meanings underlying someone's interaction with the group.

The clown

A member may adopt this role either to defend against anxiety or close relationships, or to conceal social unease. Once again, understanding the meaning of this behaviour is the key to deciding how best to respond. Enabling individuals to explore other ways of behaving and relating may require a combination of naming and discussing possible meanings in the group, practising different forms of interaction, and allocating specific group tasks such as summarising.

Subgroups

The development of subgroups may indicate apprehension about meaningful involvement in the group or disagreement with the task. They may indicate that the group has yet to find an effective means of working as a group. Consequently, Doel and Sawdon (1999b) advise reflection on the need for security within the group. Alternatively, whether formed around people or ideas, and when not opposing the group's objectives (Douglas, 2000), subgroups can generate ideas and promote the group's cohesion by involving isolated or quieter members who may find it difficult to contribute in the larger group. As such they can be a means of putting members in touch with each other and of generating discussion or activity. However, where subgroups have rigid boundaries and exclude other members, they are unlikely to promote the group's effectiveness. If groupworkers have not deliberately formed subgroups as part of the group's work, they need to understand and interpret the meaning behind their formation and discuss with members their effect on the group.

Dependency on leaders

In some groups, for example with children, groupworkers may retain responsibility for creating and maintaining the group's framework, aims and boundaries. However, although dependent to some extent on the type of group, groupworkers should seek to transfer gradually to the group responsibility for its functioning. One rationale for this approach is that many members will have resources to facilitate the group and that, if groupworkers remain central, this may deskill these members. Another rationale is that, if members can develop these skills within the group, there is an increased likelihood that the gains made therein will be sustained outside it when the group has terminated and the groupworkers' support is no longer available. However, it is a difficult task. It requires groupworkers to keep pace with and support the use of members' skills and development. Further, members may perceive the groupworkers as holding the leadership function and a position of experts, in addition to which they may be familiar with occupying a subordinate, passive position. Finally, members may reject greater involvement in facilitating the group, and the help it provides, because this may ultimately lead to task accomplishment or problem resolution and, therefore, 'loss'.

If indeed groupworkers are aiming to become less central to the group, they should make this explicit, and refer to the group rather than jump immediately in when decisions about direction and development are required. They should find ways to draw out members' resources as well as responsibilities, reviewing periodically their roles with members and the group's increasing resources to use and direct the group purposefully.

One particular form of dependency (Bion, 1961) arises when the group experiences difficulty with its task and with the emotions it triggers. The group seeks protection and support from a leader who is perceived as omnipotent and dependable. Other feelings, such as inadequacy, envy and guilt, are concealed until disappointment emerges with the leader, whereupon the group might fragment.

Conflict between members or with groupworkers

Members may express frustration with or hostility towards one another. They may ridicule or disagree with each other's suggestions. They may dispute groupworkers' suggestions and devalue the group's potential effectiveness. Once again, this phenomenon may arise when the group experiences the task as impossible (Bion, 1961). Everything is split into good and bad, with dominant emotions being fear and suspicion. Alternatively the conflict may symbolise the search for status within the group. Members may feel loyal to outside systems, such as family members or peers, whose interests or demands conflict with the group's aims.

However, conflict is not necessarily negative. It may highlight members' involvement in the group's task. It may represent impatience or disagreement with current approaches to and solutions for the group's goals. Thus, groupworkers should work with, not against, conflict (Lordan, 1996). It may offer an opportunity, for example to move beyond anger and blame to learning from the encounter with different perspectives.

Skills and roles

Facilitative groupwork maintains a balance between task achievement and the pace of work since, if members feel that the costs of membership exceed the gains, they may withdraw. Similarly, initial motivation may diminish for a time if members sense that the group's work may be difficult. A sense of stuckness may mean that the group's aims or methods of achieving them are unclear, or that dynamics within the group are preoccupying members and inhibiting engagement with tasks. The task, or achieving goals, and process, becoming and sustaining a group, must be held in balance (Brown, 1997; Lizzio and Wilson, 2001; Braye and Preston-Shoot, 2005).

This illustrates the importance of openness to what is going on and to the emotional meaning and impact of what is happening. It illustrates too the skill of balance – when to hold to boundaries and to set limits and structures, and when to be flexible because an emerging theme or issue is important or because rigid enforcement of a programme might feel like a rejection to some members (Papell, 1999; Springer *et al.*, 1999). If groupworkers focus only on task, relationships will wither and possibly become destructive. If they focus predominantly on process, little will ultimately be accomplished.

Facilitative groupwork also seeks to make available resources that members bring. This involves judgement about how much groupworkers should use their experience or expertise (Doel and Sawdon, 1999b). For instance, personal disclosure or the giving of information and opinions by groupworkers may offer encouragement and stimulate interaction but too much may be experienced as an imposition or as disempowering, or blur the boundaries between them and members (Mistry, 1989). The challenge here is one of position – central or marginal – in relation to both group task and maintenance needs. For example, Mistry (1989), working with women offenders, describes how groupworkers were initially active in introducing topics but, as the group developed, members increasingly offered ideas and were able to challenge each other. Braye and Preston-Shoot (2005) also found members more prepared to challenge each other as the group sensed a safe environment. Initially groupworkers may offer their knowledge about a topic (Hill, 2001) but increasingly may be able to draw awareness from others (Vernelle, 1994).

This centre/edge dynamic arises when considering how to mobilise the group's resources to enable members to support each other and work effectively together. Habermann (1993) refers to the gradual abrogation of control but this requires judgement about the group's movement away from dependence. In formed groups this may be difficult when members have emotional needs for which they envisage the groupworkers as sources of help and security. Group members may become confused and angry if workers withdraw prematurely, that is, before members have developed trust in each other and recognised their authority of expertise and knowledge. In peer-led and self-directed groups facilitators are already in a different position. They may offer their knowledge and experience but the group is responsible for decisions about task and maintenance (Schneewind, 1996). In all groups, to varying degrees at different times, groupworkers need skills in helping members establish and pursue goals, decide how the group is to be conducted and reflect on whether processes are helping or hindering task accomplishment, and in spotting themes, energies, ideas and blocks (Mullender and Ward, 1989).

Another angle on the centre/edge dynamic is the degree to which a groupworker is or is not a group member. Without some professional distance groupworkers cannot be effective facilitators (Groves and Schondel, 1997/98) or change agents. Too much and they may become divorced from group needs (Bensted *et al.*, 1994). Yet another angle is the degree to which the group or individual members are central. Sometimes the group may want to emphasise what connects members; sometimes it will need flexibility to address the variety of problems, needs and issues concerning individuals. A skill here is that of positioning, to be able to use the excitement of difference (Lordan, 1996), which is generated by experiencing different meanings and perspectives, to enable members as individuals and as a group to find room for manoeuvre and metanoia – a shift of mind. Enabling others to see an issue from a different vantage point, moving them figuratively or actually to a new position from which to view something, or reframing to broaden a perspective, all introduce new possibilities.

An effective group needs groupworkers and members who have skills and roles to move the work forward and to maintain the setting as positive and creative. Ideally both groupworkers and members will be drawing on observation and assessment in order to determine how and where to intervene. The intervention may be holding on to sensitive issues or difficult topics and not retreating into safer arenas, or holding on to tensions and differences until these can be resolved or integrated into the group's understanding. Alternatively the intervention may be designed to release group resources. One role here is encouraging and supporting members to explore their concerns. People may not always realise when they are helping others (Hopmeyer and Werk, 1993) so reinforcing their helpful interventions may boost their self-esteem. It may also promote learning.

The intervention may focus on group climate and culture. Skills and roles here include eliciting – seeking information or clarification, and identifying people's goals (Lizzio and Wilson, 2001) – and integrating, using reflection to summarise and pull together before moving forward. Using empathy and respect will help to communicate understanding, acceptance and valuation of what people offer. Skills in bringing people in, involving others, may promote interaction. There may be a role for harmonising, bringing about compromise and resolution, but also for challenging and reality-based, controlled expression of feelings such as anger (Malekoff, 1999; Ward and Mullender, 1991) since these can ultimately lead away from superficiality to a more informed comprehension. Without challenge there can be little learning (Breton, 1991; Doel and Sawdon, 1999b).

Process and task may both be addressed by building – opening up or developing contributions and issues can bring people closer together or to a new understanding (Malekoff, 1999; Braye and Preston-Shoot, 2005). It can keep communication smooth and open (Ward and Mullender, 1991) and help people work collectively. Process and task can both be addressed also by the expression of curiosity, to facilitate critical thinking. Expressed curiosity may focus on what is happening, what is influencing this, and what it is like for group members, individually and collectively. It may focus on how the task is being developed, whether solutions are enabling or more dysfunctional in work terms, and whether some options are being overlooked.

The intervention may be designed to stimulate work. Skills and roles here include introducing ideas, making proposals, or declaring difference. They include testing understanding and consensus since it is too easy to reach a conclusion without resolving conflict that may lie beneath (Doel and Sawdon, 1999b). Groupworkers and members may check out their observations, revealing their thinking and highlighting how themes or behaviours are shaping the group (Douglas, 2000). Sharing feelings and understanding can help the group make sense of what is happening, especially when related to evidence within it (Turkie, 1992) but timing and phraseology are important. Observation, especially when coupled with interpretation, may enlarge a group's understanding, although it may also generate uncomfortable feelings and resistance or denial (Fitzsimmons and Levy, 1996), which will need to be held or contained until they can be assimilated. Equally, understanding or learning cannot be imposed but, rather, must be experienced. Thus, patience and tolerance of uncertainty are key attributes. It may be difficult to know, especially early on in a group (Papell, 1999), how meaningful a theme or issue is to members. The meaning of behaviour may not be apparent, illustrating the need to hold these things in mind, possibly to return to them later.

Conclusion

Working with groups provides groupworkers with learning opportunities but can also be stressful when they experience the power of group dynamics, encounter difficulties which cloud the way forward, or doubt the effectiveness of their work. The next two chapters aim to provide structures which, in addition to those already discussed, can enable groupworkers to work through difficulties and extend the boundaries of what groupwork can achieve for members and groupworkers alike.

8 | Supervision

Introduction

The code of conduct for employers (GSCC, 2002) requires that agencies must manage and supervise staff to support effective practice. Interest in promoting learning organisations has accompanied this statutory confirmation of the centrality of supervision to social (care) work. This chapter's philosophy is that supervision is indeed essential for effective groupwork yet it is relatively neglected within the literature.

Supervision and consultation

Some writers refer to consultation rather than supervision. Mullender and Ward (1989) identify a consultant as someone who assists groupworkers prepare. The consultant models self-directed groupwork by providing a framework for discussions rather than determining their content. Henchman and Walton (1997/98) found consultants helpful, especially in teams where questioning and positive challenge were not the norm. Working with male offenders, consultancy was found to sharpen up practice. It helped groupworkers to be clear about the relationship between masculinity and crime, and improved their ability to communicate about the group to practitioner and manager colleagues (Bensted *et al.*, 1994). As a result their work became recognised and supported.

Reynolds and Shackman (1994) suggest that consultants should have skills and experience of relevance and resonance to the groupworkers' practice. Groupworkers and consultants should take responsibility for the effective use of their time together. Mistry and Brown (1991) suggest that consultation is especially important when groupworkers are inexperienced, when issues of 'race' and ethnicity might inhibit communication within the group and between groupworkers, and when understanding and using group process are particularly important.

A consultation network can offer a secure base for group-workers committed to developing anti-oppressive groupwork practice (Preston-Shoot, 1992). The network allows groupworkers to share ideas for establishing and maintaining groupwork in agencies, for promoting partnership and empowerment as an organisational issue, and for responding to themes emerging in their work. The network supports groupworkers as they implement strategies for researching service user and colleague definitions of issues, for making links with key managers and for stimulating groupwork practice.

Groups typically lack a consultancy or supervisory framework (Mullender, 1996). Whether continuing professional development is provided within or outside a line management context, the reasons for exploring practice with a third person are the same, even for experienced groupworkers.

Why supervision?

> ### putting into practice: exploring the value of supervision
>
> Take a situation with which you are working and about which you are concerned. Using a consultant and live supervision team, review your work, especially focusing on your concerns and the approaches you have adopted to try to resolve them. After twenty minutes, consider as a group:
>
> ➤ What processes were helpful or unhelpful.
> ➤ The experiences of all those involved.
> ➤ What was happening in the group and what information this might provide about the situation.
> ➤ What hypotheses have emerged about the concerns and the approaches used to tackle them, which it might be helpful to explore further.

The demands of leadership/facilitation

Reid (1988) describes fears and fantasies surrounding leading groups. These include competitive struggles with group members, or attributing group events such as silence to one's own approach. Leaders may fear rejection or opprobrium if they challenge or confront members. In response practitioners may adopt defensive manoeuvres and security operations, such as withdrawing psychologically from the group to avoid any emotional impact on them, accentuating authority and difference, or attempting to exercise tight control. Supervision enables groupworkers to reflect on such 'what if?' situations.

When practitioners are planning groups, supervision enables them to debrief and to keep focused (Nosko and Breton, 1997/98). When groupworkers are leading, it enables them to learn from someone else's perspectives, to clarify their aims, to develop their programme, to explore group dynamics, and to determine how to respond to group members based on an understanding of their needs (Lebacq and Shah, 1989). It also provides a space through which to negotiate transition out of the group (Malekoff, 1999). In short, supervision can help leaders/facilitators explore their involvement in the group, retain clear aims, discover their resources for understanding and using the group's dynamics and process, manage anxieties, and maintain enthusiasm and direction.

For co-workers, supervision is essential for working together effectively, a space in which to explore roles, styles of work, perspectives and conflicts, and to understand and develop the relationship. Co-leadership is a complex relationship of central importance in the group. Like any relationship, difficulties may arise which, if not resolved, may prove counterproductive for the partnership and the group's dynamics and task accomplishment. Co-workers may become competitive, undermine each other in the search for acceptance by the group, or collude with each other against or with the group. The distribution of tasks may be uneven or roles may become rigid rather than changing in line with developments in the group or in the leaders' confidence and skills.

The demands of groupwork

putting into practice: the dynamics within the work

When working with groups, what roles and tasks do you find particularly difficult or stressful? What might be contributing to these feelings? What defences have you adopted? What might enable you to hold more effectively to the task?

When groupwork is proving difficult, one line of enquiry is the groupworker's own contribution (Vernelle, 1994). Groupworkers may ignore or encourage certain individual and group behaviours and processes because of their own needs, which may impede their effectiveness in enabling individuals and the group to address the issues that have brought them together. Schiller (2003) argues that groupworkers' awareness of their own process is critical – their biases, beliefs, relationship with conflict and anger, and the strategies they have developed in response. Similarly, Mullender and Ward (1991) highlight the difficulty in self-directed groupwork for facilitators to resist group pressure to be directive. They also acknowledge the possible intrusion of groupworkers' own preferences into judgements about what a group may need. Supervision then offers a safe space that acts as a container in which emotional disturbance may be felt and learned from (Tribe, 1997/98).

Initially, at least, groupworkers may experience considerable anxiety about whether the group will come together and work effectively on its agreed tasks. Defensive reactions may easily become prominent, therefore, perhaps in the form of finding it difficult to allow members time to form gradually into a cohesive group and to not over-plan the group. Why supervision? One answer is because work engenders feelings that, if not managed, will resurface, possibly destructively. It is a forum in which workers can identify their anxieties or concerns, and explore how they might maximise the potential of the group and of themselves.

Issues in groupwork

Mistry (1989), reviewing a feminist groupwork model, identifies the issue of maintaining an appropriate professional stance. Similarly, Pease (2003) and Mullender (1996) both identify the dangers of collusion, for instance when male practitioners are working with perpetrators of domestic violence. Gobat (1993) highlights the potential difficulty of managing powerful, expressed emotions and the urge in response towards cohesion where the leader becomes one of the group. Supervision should prove helpful when boundaries between groupworkers and members are becoming blurred, when there are processes involving members and groupworkers to be understood. If practitioners feel enmeshed, over-involved or overwhelmed in the group, the more detached view of the supervisor might help the groupworkers to clarify what is happening in the group and how they might intervene effectively.

Supervision is a useful forum for discussing practice-related questions. It may be concerned with how to handle termination and manage any feelings that the group's work remains incomplete. It may be concerned with enabling groupworkers to reflect on their experience of the group and what they have learned. When groupworkers are planning, supervision may assist them in deciding the type, length and membership of the group, or in negotiating entry into a preexisting group and helping its members to define the issues to be tackled. Supervision may help to clarify whether the group should be concerned with work with individuals in a group format, focusing on individual members' problems, or with systems within which group members exist. In other words, are the goals individual-centred or aiming for social change? During the group the leaders may welcome support in coping with the members' expression of powerful emotions and in finding ways to involve them in commenting on the effectiveness of the group. Throughout, the supervisor can be a source of support, someone who enables the workers to clarify their roles and goals, and the extent to which their actions are promoting the group's aims. It offers a second opinion on risk-taking and innovation. It is a forum for formulating and reviewing strategy, and maintaining a consistent approach over time.

Monitoring of the work

---

putting into practice: the complexity of the work

Take a group you are working with. What pressures are there on you? What tensions and practice dilemmas exist? From where do these pressures spring? How might your responses be functional or dysfunctional? What next steps do you plan and why?

Fitzsimmons and Levy (1996) found that regular supervision of an art therapy group for young people with eating disorders was extremely supportive. It facilitated a clear focus on key issues emerging from the material and group dynamics, including powerful transference and counter-transference. Effective supervision also offers a holding function when groupworkers encounter doubt or fear, risk and ambiguity. Supervision is also a reflective space where groupworkers can consider the meaning of events and behaviours in this group's context (Malekoff, 1999).

Supervision is a means of ensuring accountability. This covers the statutory obligations, policies and standards of the agency sponsoring the groupwork, ensuring that the groupworkers adhere to these, but also supporting the leaders/facilitators in their attempts to change an agency's approach and attitudes towards a particular client group. The supervisor may help to ensure that the agency is aware of changing needs, is in touch with members' views and circumstances, and remains responsive. Supervision also covers the progress, outcomes and quality of the work. The supervisor needs to be aware of what occurs in the group in order to help groupworkers assess whether the power of the group is rendering them ineffective or exposing the group and some of its members to possible harm. The supervisor may comment on the progress of a co-work relationship and of the group, where necessary focusing on difficulties or challenges and helping groupworkers to decide what action to take, when and how.

Professional development

---

putting into practice: the dynamics within workers

Identify the sad, angry, abusive (if any) experiences associated with social (care) work and/or supervision. In what ways have these experiences been carried over, either by repetition or determined attempts at correction, into your practice?

Supervision allows practitioners to deal with those parts of their own experience and learning that may block development of their work (Vernelle, 1994). It is a space for reflection and for enhancing practice (Tribe, 1997/98), for learning from mistakes (Malekoff, 1999). Social (care) workers carry high levels of responsibility, face complex demands, and frequently feel overburdened and under siege. Supervision has a symbolic value since it represents a commitment to professional development. It also has a pragmatic purpose, that of enabling groupworkers to consolidate and extend their knowledge and skills by helping them to specify what they are bringing to each task, to evaluate their effectiveness, and to illustrate what learning they might transfer from groupwork into other settings.

Choice of supervisor

In many agencies there is an absence of choice. However, wherever possible, thinking through allocation of supervision is advisable. Lebacq and Shah (1989), for example, omitted to consider formal input from a black consultant, which made it difficult for them to consider the effects of racism on the group. On reflection they identified the need for individual and shared sessions with a focus on white worker racism and black worker responses to it, which would have required a level of trust, familiarity and openness about the power dynamics between the workers.

---

putting into practice: choosing a supervisor

Groupworkers and potential supervisor Identify their previous experiences of supervision, including what they found helpful, difficult but beneficial, and unhelpful. They should also list what they regard as constructive and inappropriate approaches to giving and receiving supervision. Finally, they should describe how they approach new learning, their learning styles.

These lists can then be reviewed in order to establish whether a contract for working together appears viable.

There is no guarantee that a supervisory relationship will meet groupworkers' needs. Counterproductive difficulties may emerge, demonstrated perhaps in communication difficulties, possibly because the groupworkers and supervisor have different learning styles and perspectives about appropriate methods of supervision. Previous experiences of supervision may also complicate the negotiation of new arrangements since, whether or not these were felt to be helpful or unsatisfactory, their legacy will be influential. They will shape what the participants bring to the new encounter, feelings that should be acknowledged and worked through if they are not to frustrate time together.

There is also a variety of roles which supervisors may adopt, and a variety of foci for the sessions. Failure to agree on the content of supervision sessions and to clarify what kind of supervision is required and available may mean the supervisor conducting sessions based on previous experience, which may be out of place in this context, or on assumptions about what the groupworkers are expecting or will find useful. The co-workers may present for supervision what they assume the supervisor expects, again reflecting the operation of implicit assumptions. Key questions then revolve around what groupworkers want from supervision and what roles they are looking for from the supervisor with which the supervisor feels comfortable. It may be helpful here for supervisors to share with groupworkers their assessment of their strengths, weaknesses and skills, and for the groupworkers to provide potential supervisors with a job description and some details about the proposed group, the stage of any co-work relationship, and their confidence as individual groupworkers. This will provide a basis for ensuring that roles are clear. If the purpose is clear, supervisors should know whether they possess the knowledge and expertise to help the groupworkers practise effectively. If it is unclear, there is an increased likelihood that expectations will be disappointed and that difficulties or important issues will be neglected.

The supervisor and groupworkers may hold divergent views about groupwork. Discongruent theoretical models can inhibit the usefulness of the supervisory process, frustrating communication and connections between practice and theory. Additionally, there must exist the potential for trust if supervision is to address effectively the demands and issues inherent in groupwork practice. This trust will be fostered if the participants share similar approaches to learning and practice, and if agreement is established concerning the extent to which supervision is to focus on group dynamics, the co-work relationship, groupwork techniques or wider issues of the systems with which the group is interacting.

Thereafter there are some practical issues to be resolved. First, can a regular time slot be found and is agreement possible on the frequency of sessions? What is to be the duration of the contract between the groupworkers and supervisor? Groupworkers need to determine what they feel to be a desirable frequency and time commitment. Ideally, supervision meetings should follow shortly after each group meeting when the events of the group will still be uppermost in leaders' minds. Lebacq and Shah (1989) found that consultation monthly proved too big a gap after critical group sessions. Supervisors must be certain that they can meet the demands for time made on them and that they have their own support systems available.

Second, supervision should begin before the group's first meeting since it is important to focus on the early stages of a co-work relationship, on preparation of the group, and on the tuning-in process of supervisor and workers. This relationship needs as much preparation as the group. Early sessions may be characterised by reticence. Time may be required to enable the participants to move beyond support and encouragement to offering challenging or critical comments. Time may also be necessary to dispel myths or fears within supervision: for example, either that the supervisor's style will smother the emerging styles of the groupworkers, or that the supervisor is an omniscient expert.

Third, the co-workers may not know the supervisor equally well. Where the supervisor of one of the co-workers is to supervise the partnership, it is important to pay some attention to the change in roles and to devote some time to becoming acquainted. The use of personal profiles may prove helpful here, both to provide personal details and to enable the participants to see what is available within the relationship.

Fourth, just as co-work partnerships and groups pass through a variety of stages, so too does a supervisory relationship. Broadly, the relationship will be marked by phases of coming together, embarking on the task, revision and possibly redefinition of the task and the relationship, and maturation. The most important phase when considering the relationship at the outset is that of revision. It is essential to build the concept of revision into the structure of the relationship, to set time aside for considering the extent to which supervision is meeting the groupworkers' needs. This may help the participants to raise areas of dissatisfaction and thereby enable the process to be more productive.

Next, consideration should be given to the format for conducting the sessions. How will the agenda be established? Will material be submitted beforehand? When groupworkers are co-working, will the supervisor offer sessions to individual practitioners? This may be appropriate for students and practitioners new to group-work. However, if adopted, there will need to be some mechanism whereby learning achieved in individual sessions can be incorporated into their joint working. Where a groupworker is running more than one group with different co-workers, is each group to have its own supervisor, will one supervisor cover each group or is it desirable for the supervisor to meet with all the groupworkers in group supervision? Decisions here depend very much on the confidence of the supervisor and groupworkers, and on whether there are sufficient similarities between the groups. The last option, meeting with all groupworkers together, offers added value in that they may experience what it is like to be a group member, to experience and to take on leadership functions, and to see from a different perspective how task and process might be balanced.

Lastly, decisions will need to be made concerning the supervisor's authority. Is it expected that the supervisor will use their authority to sanction activities and to ensure that the work is consistent with the goals and expectations of the agency, or is their role that of sharing knowledge, skills and expertise? In other words, does the supervisor's position within the agency mean that they are accountable for the groupworkers' practice? This is even more relevant when co-workers are members of different teams or organisations. Here the limits of the supervisor should be delineated clearly and decisions taken concerning the amount of reporting back to those teams or agencies.

Once these negotiations have been concluded, the agreements can be recorded in a written contract. This should set out clearly the structure, frequency and purpose of meetings, and the roles that the supervisor is to adopt.

The focus and content of supervision

The focus and content of supervision will be determined by the phase that the groupworkers and group have reached. Broadly there are four stages. Stage one is marked by personal preparation, which to some degree will overlap with stage two. This involves preparation to work with a group. Issues relating to leading/facilitating the group, and maintaining themselves as resource figures, occur in the third stage, while evaluation and termination of the group form the final phase.

Inevitably, in deciding the agenda for supervision, practitioners will face the question of priorities, especially the choice between depth and breadth. There are also pressure points to be aware of. Groupworkers may find it easier to raise issues relating to the group, or practical matters, rather than those relating to themselves and their co-working relationship. This may be because the former are more accessible and less threatening. However, groupwork's effectiveness depends on self-awareness and on the viability of co-work partnerships. Accordingly, this should be thoroughly discussed in supervision. Tribe (1997/98) recommends that spaces be reserved for practical issues, perhaps towards the end of a meeting, in order to keep focus on the emotional terrain and the psychological implications of the work.

Supervisors should be careful not to stunt the spontaneity of the groupworkers by making them too self-conscious or by offering too many comments of what they would have done (Yalom, 1995). Suggestions can all too easily be turned into the only way to approach groupwork, losing the essential connection between the groupworkers' understanding of this group's process and content and their resources in terms of styles and strengths. Enabling groupworkers to engage with their practice can be achieved in several ways. They might be asked to spontaneously report on their work, with the supervisor alert to what is or is not discussed, how the work is described and the issues constructed, and to the possibility that the supervisory process may be mirroring some aspect of the groupwork itself. A particular dilemma, choice point or critical incident might be unpacked, or a step-by-step account given of a groupwork encounter, with subsequent discussion of surrounding emotions, underlying theory, and how to consolidate any learning.

Since an infinite number of situations can arise in the course of planning and running a group, it is helpful if the supervisor knows in advance what the groupworkers wish to discuss and has a written summary of the group and the groupworkers' preparatory discussions or post-group reflections. This will help the supervisor to tune in.

Stage one: becoming a groupworker (again)

Individual issues can impede a worker's professional development and a co-work partnership. An early task for the supervisor is to enable groupworkers to:

● Relate past experiences to the present, envisaged task.
● Consider how their styles and value base might influence their approach to and goals for the intended group.
● Discuss expectations about co-working, groupwork and supervision and their links to knowledge and experiences within groups.
● Identify strengths so that these might be available for the group.

Knowledge may include training and also learning derived from research and from work with experts by experience. Feelings may involve articulating fears, fantasies and assumptions, which need to be worked through to release creative work. Groupworkers may doubt their groupwork skills. Their practice can be facilitated through making explicit their strengths and resources, such as the knowledge gained from membership of many different groups. Essentially the focus here is intrapersonal development, enhancing their ability to understand their own and other people's movement in and around groups. How does this groupworker make sense of their practice? How might this impact on group dynamics, on others involved in groupwork? The focus is not just on their practice but on who they are and the qualities they bring to their tasks, whether inspirational, empathetic, motivational, confident, nurturing, commitment or whatever.

When co-working there are additional interpersonal issues to consider. Each practitioner will have ideas about the strengths, hopes, fears, advantages and difficulties in the partnership. They may find it easier to discuss the positives, what the relationship offers them and the group, and the supervisor may have to encourage the groupworkers to express any personal anxieties or problems encountered. Co-workers may be reluctant to mention anything that they find irritating in order not to jeopardise the relationship or proposed groupwork. However, concerns raised and handled sensitively should strengthen rather than undermine working together. What is important is that any difficulties or fears

are not minimised since they have a direct bearing on the effectiveness of co-work. Equally, the positives should be carefully
examined, for example validating where mutual respect allows the
creative use of differences and can model a positive interpersonal
relationship for group members. A supervisor can help practitioners to express their hopes, test out whether the relationship can
meet these expectations, and examine whether these positives are
being emphasised in order to minimise or deny difficulties. Accordingly, the supervisor's tasks might include focusing on:

- Issues or dynamics between co-workers which they might be
  overlooking, such as a partnership based on feelings of
  personal weakness and where the workers discount themselves.
- Identifying and examining their expectations, needs and
  problems within the partnership.
- Identifying and stressing their mutuality so that the stability of
  their partnership might be enhanced.
- Mobilising strengths by drawing out past learning and
  connecting skills and knowledge used in contexts outside the
  group.

Supervision should also focus on the groupworkers' theoretical
orientation, their manner of handling and identifying problems, and
the balance of their contribution to their working together, perhaps
using exercises described in Chapter 6. Coupled with reflection on
their use of supervision, on their own preparatory discussions and
on their efforts at planning their groupwork, this focus will offer
an understanding of how open and trusting co-workers are with
each other and the supervisor. It will become apparent whether they
compete for attention and whether there is any conflict or collusion
between them. Supervision may mirror their interaction within the
partnership generally, for example in who defers and who reports.
Ultimately, is there a workable balance between their similarities
and differences? What problems or difficulties should be resolved
for the co-workers to be effective? The supervisor is concerned with
developing rapport between the co-workers. Where the supervisor
assists groupworkers to overcome difficulties, they may gain confidence in the process approach to problem resolution. This may
prove valuable in the group. Neglect of the co-workers' relationship may make for problems for the practitioners within the
group.

Stage two: preparing for groupwork

Where a proposed group is only a blueprint, the supervisor may assist the groupworkers in formulating a proposal that responds to the needs being presented to the agency. The supervisor may be a resource figure at this point, possessing knowledge about the agency and the demands any particular client group presents to it. Alternatively, the supervisor may assist groupworkers to research and map need before devising possible aims and objectives for a group. The task is to share in devising a basic framework that focuses on:

● The general interests and areas of work that practitioners are seeking for experience.
● Specifying the purpose of the group, ensuring that aims are realistic.
● Deciding the type of group and the methods to be used.
● Specifying the theoretical bases from which practitioners work and highlighting whether their knowledge and experience need to be supplemented through research or training.

Thereafter there are questions of membership, referrals, frequency and duration to be resolved. The supervisor may be able to assist the groupworkers plan groupwork that is realistic in terms of their other commitments and then to present their project and understand and cope with (negative) reactions from colleagues. The supervisor's knowledge of the organisation may prove useful in clarifying and then ensuring good liaison between groupworkers and the agency concerning (Hodge, 1985):

● Access to and provision of recording and reports.
● Consultation with managers.
● Confidentiality and information exchange between groupworkers and colleagues about group members, for example when referrals are sought or on termination of the group.
● Who holds accountability for the agency's involvement with a group member.
● To whom groupworkers are accountable, particularly when they work for different organisations.

On accountability for work with individual group members, groupworkers, their practitioner and manager colleagues, and the supervisor should reflect on the advantages and drawbacks of different arrangements (Manor, 1989). There may be risks to be managed. Who holds accountability for an agency's involvement may affect how individuals engage with the group. Where individuals have complex needs involving several practitioners, what will best promote coordinated activity?

Preparing to engage with an existing group covers some of the same ground, such as ensuring clarity about accountability and confidentiality, and reflecting on the fit between what groupworkers might offer and what group members are looking for. Whatever the group, supervision can also imagine problems that may arise and ways of handling them, the division of roles for the groupworkers both within the group and between sessions, and how work with the group might be organised so as to meet its objectives.

Stage three: working with a group

One focus here for supervision will be the group. Exactly what is discussed will be influenced by the group's purposes but one emphasis will be on increasing the groupworkers' awareness of the group's process and on developing their interpersonal skills and professional expertise. The supervisor may achieve this by offering constructive criticism and support, by encouraging self-criticism and evaluation, and by reassuring workers of the universality of the experience of understanding one's activity without necessarily feeling able to control it. Useful questions include:

- How is the group progressing towards achieving its aims? What developments in the group are contributing towards this progression and what are impeding it? What part are the groupworkers playing here?
- Is any revision of the group's aims or length necessary?
- Is the group's programme helpful to what the group is trying to achieve?
- What particular problems have arisen between members or between groupworkers and members? How might these be dealt with?
- What theoretical frameworks help to make sense of the group's development and dynamics? How might these be incorporated into the groupworkers' practice?

● Are the leaders' styles facilitating the group? Are co-workers participating equally or are their feelings towards the group, the members or each other impeding their interaction with the group? Is their behaviour congruent with their feelings and the group's process?

Groupworkers may experience strong and confusing feelings (Malekoff, 1999), the origin of which should be explored. They may be a reaction to particular members or issues. What group-workers have taken into the group from family roles or previous personal and/or work experiences may trigger them. Groupworkers may find it difficult to tolerate the expression of powerful emotions, perhaps fearing group disintegration or hostility, which their responses may further compound. Where practitioners are unaware of their own needs and the influence they can have, they may respond to them and unduly distort required work. Consequently, there should be some focus on personal awareness. This aims to increase a groupworker's understanding of their own behaviour and its effect on group members, and of the impact of group members on them. Some focus may become appropriate on a worker's security operations, the roles adopted to cope with the group experience (Williams, 1966). If a worker experiences the need to control, to avoid self-exposure, or to be liked, supervision may help the practitioner to understand the fears or dynamics underlying these roles, enable them to reassess what they experience, and to respond more appropriately to the group's needs.

A continued focus on co-working, where appropriate, will ensure its continued effectiveness within the group. Again, group dynamics may trigger issues for the co-workers. These could include increasing competitiveness, anxiety about letting one's partner down, concern about differences in leadership style, or difficulties about agreeing a way forward. Perhaps because it seems threatening, some practitioners may not wish to discuss in supervision dynamics between co-workers, preferring to discuss the strengths and similarities in the relationship. The supervisor will have to create a holding, safe environment to facilitate expression of the more dissatisfying aspects of co-working.

Whether focusing on the groupworkers or on the group, the supervisor's role is to listen, question, test impressions and draw out any conflict (Mullender and Ward, 1989). The supervisor takes

responsibility for creating a learning environment and invites exploration but ultimately the groupworkers must find their own way
through the demands and challenges presented by the group. The
supervisor may use direct observation and feedback from group
members, or may ask groupworkers to keep and share a diary or
learning log about the group.

Stage four: evaluation and termination

Supervisors can assist groupworkers to evaluate the outcome of the
group and their practice, to identify what they have learned and to
disseminate their observations to colleagues. They may help them
to identify their feelings related to group endings. Feelings such as
denial and loss may be evoked and should be worked through, as
well as thinking about ending rituals that capture the emotional
power of the group (Ross, 1991) and enable everyone to find personal bridges across to a new situation, one without this group.

Learning organisations

Doel (2006) observes that supervisors may prove effective advocates
for groupwork becoming part of an organisation's mainstream provision. Doel and Sawdon (1999b), in order to establish groupwork
in an agency, recommend a learning-organisation strategy in order
to accumulate and consolidate experience. Pease (2003) also refers
to a learning community, which can subject its own values and priorities to scrutiny, can theorise from experience, and can critique the
context in which groups operate. A needs analysis, and reflection
prompted by outcomes from groupwork and other interventions,
can be used to inform an action plan that clearly articulates desired
goals and means of achieving them. The action plan is the learning
community's expression of a shared vision generated from a flow of
information, dialogue, consultation and shared decision-making. As
with groups, the hallmarks of a learning organisation include relationships that can be non-hierarchical, based on respect and involvement, and an atmosphere of trust where everything that occurs is
seen as an opportunity for growth.

Group supervision could operate as a learning community, cap-
turing and disseminating into an organisation and its environment
learning from groupwork. For example, Ward (1995) found that

group supervision enabled staff in a children's home to explore feelings and thoughts about their work. Individual supervision proved insufficient for dealing with the range of issues confronted by the team. Supervisors can contribute to the agency as a learning organisation by reporting on its suitability as a work environment and by attempting to address shortcomings in its response to research-informed propositions.

Further value of group supervision resides in the experience it provides of group membership for groupworkers. It enables them to feel something of what people they work with experience (Lordan, 1996), to experience different styles of leadership (Vernelle, 1994), and to learn about their responses to group dynamics. Group supervision also provides an opportunity for groupworkers to deal with those experiences which may block the development of their work (Vernelle, 1994). They can hold a mirror to their own behaviour and (cultural or gender) inheritance (Bensted *et al.*, 1994) which, if unexplored, may lead them through such processes as counter-transference to collude with group members, or to push too hard for change, or to look for safety rather than purposeful work.

Conclusion

Supervision is not an easy undertaking. Group issues may impact directly on it through mirroring. Issues between group members and between groupworkers and members can be played out between groupworkers and supervisor (Mullender and Ward, 1989). Supervisors may find themselves favouring one of the workers or allocating a senior role to one when this has not been agreed, which could be reflective of tensions requiring exploration. It requires commitment, sensitivity, strength and perseverance, especially when the supervisor perceives issues that need to be tackled but which groupworkers are avoiding. There are also questions of assessment and appraisal, which loom large for students but probably are crucial to all workers when focusing on learning and professional development. It will be apparent, therefore, that supervisors need a variety of skills:

- Advocacy for the groupworkers and group.
- Collaboration in problem-solving and providing suggestions concerning possible approaches to problems and issues.

- Provision of knowledge.
- Staying meta (Preston-Shoot and Agass, 1990) to what is happening – how is supervision being used and what does this say about the group and groupworkers? How is this group being presented (for instance, clearly, chaotically, with detachment or over-involvement) and why might this be? What is the supervisor being asked for and what does this say?
- Reflecting back, enabling the development of understanding, the processing of feelings and the thinking through of what is happening.
- Commentary on processes and communication within the group or between groupworkers, identifying and exploring themes and underlying topics, for instance anger towards one member or conflict between groupworkers that is revealed in supervision interactions.
- Linking groupworkers' practice within this group to their work generally, to increase the possibility of transferring knowledge and skills from one context to another.
- Facilitation, helping groupworkers to identify themes and problems and to work towards solutions for themselves.

When supervisors feel comfortable with this variety of roles and when practitioners feel congenial with their supervisor, the process can be very useful. Indeed, working with groups is inadvisable when supervision is not available.

9 | Evaluating and researching groupwork practice

Introduction

This chapter will survey evaluation in groupwork practice, argue for strengthening the evidencing of groupwork and offer tools for researching more systematically what makes groups work. Effective evaluation is difficult (Towl and Dexter, 1994). How can practitioners define and measure change, be certain that it is the direct result of groupwork, and identify what the outcomes have been for participants?

The mandates for evaluation

Evaluation is a significant part of the modernisation agenda (DH, 1998). Key benchmarks for social work and health-related services, and for probation and youth justice practice, are that provision should be characterised by:

● Standards and accountability, to ensure role clarity, consistent quality and the protection of service users from ineffective and abusive practice.
● Responsiveness and flexibility, to ensure that the needs of service users rather than the imperatives of providers are paramount.
● Inclusion and involvement, to ensure that user and carer perspectives shape service design, planning, development and evaluation.

One further benchmark is that services should be evidence-based. In terms of groupwork planning, delivery and evaluation, this suggests a focus on what value the intervention adds. Pollio (2002) identifies accountability as a prominent theme and suggests that the failure to incorporate evidence into practice is an ethical violation. Indeed, it has never been professionally desirable or ethically acceptable simply to appeal to a value base and remain unclear how groups help people, in what circumstances and for how long. Social workers have a responsibility to specify what they can do and how, to adopt a consciously evaluative attitude to their practice.

There is, as yet, little published evidence of how groupworkers are adjusting to the modernisation agenda. In fact, delivering evidence-based groupwork might prove challenging. Some writers have conceded that their approach to assessing effectiveness has been insufficiently rigorous or systematic (Cowburn, 1990; Mulvie, 1991). It is arguable too that evaluative research on outcomes of groupwork practice and groupwork's conceptual base is scarce, making it difficult, for instance, to advance groupwork as the intervention of choice or to distinguish between the merits of smaller or larger, open or closed groups. Mullender (1996) asserts that groupworkers have been insufficiently rigorous in monitoring their favoured models, in conducting follow-up and in their use of methodology.

However, evaluation can improve the quality of services by ensuring that planning and activities are directed towards purposeful outcomes, and by defining for future workers and service users what contributes to effectiveness. Groupwork contains many variables. There are the groupworkers' skills, leadership styles and qualities such as empathy. There are the nature and degree of members' difficulties, their social situations, and the extent to which they accept the group's rationale. Then there is the quality of relationships established in the group. Interrogating these variables, analysing their development in and effect on the group's outcome, may highlight those qualities that promote successful groupwork. For example, practitioners' personal, interactive style and attention to process may affect outcomes (Braye and Preston-Shoot, 2005). In defining core skills, evaluation adds substance to otherwise anecdotal accounts and clarifies where an intervention is especially effective in helping to achieve change.

Planning work with specific goals brings clarity to complicated situations. By referring back to and reviewing initial purposes through collecting information on the group's development, practitioners can establish important features that have occurred and why, and to what extent aims have been achieved. They can establish whether further areas of work exist and whether modifications to the group's goals are necessary. That is, evaluation may offer grounds for continuing groupwork or for ending positively rather than allowing the work to drift. Follow-up can develop this by providing information on whether changes are sustained and carried over by members into other settings. Results can inform future priority-setting and practice, for instance selection criteria for future groups and optimum time frames for particular problems to be tackled or aims to be achieved. Evaluation may provide practitioners with increased confidence. All this has considerable practice relevance.

The evidence of effectiveness

Locating the evidence of groupwork's value and relevance should be a core component of practice, partly in order to capture the space opened up by the social policy concern with best value. Powerful claims are indeed advanced for groupwork's potential to realise individual and social change. Groups, it is claimed (Heap, 1992; Kohli, 1993; Kurland and Salmon, 1993; Brown, 1997; Lee, 1999; Springer et al., 1999), can generate hope and dignity, provide acceptance and commonality, and offer cathartic release and solidarity. They provide settings for learning and growth, reciprocity and collective action. On balance the evidence for individual change appears stronger than that for social change, perhaps because this is the traditional focus of much professional activity. Both self-help groups and worker-facilitated groups report changes in how people perceive experiences and issues, how they feel, how they speak about and resolve issues, and how they engage with others (see, for example, Hopmeyer and Werk, 1993; Garrett, 1995; Hill, 2001). However, DeLois (2003), Mullender and Ward (1991) and Ni Chorcora et al. (1994) demonstrate that it is possible to use groupwork to promote partnership and dialogue and to effect structural change.

Nonetheless, despite numerous practitioner evaluations of groupwork's effectiveness, the current state of the research evidence appears variable in terms of demonstrating that groupwork planning, delivery and outcomes are appropriate and relevant, acceptable and equitable, effective and efficient. Concern lingers (Matzat, 1993; Hopmeyer and Werk, 1993) about a lack of research and comparative studies without which it remains difficult to evidence the claims for groupwork, to maximise its beneficial aspects and to collect data for theory-building and refinement. So how might groupwork practice provide the evidence?

Researching practice

Five knowledge drivers are available (Pawson *et al.*, 2003), utilisation of which may turn to advantage disputes about what counts as evidence. The first is the reported experience of service users and carers. This knowledge driver is not yet delivering its full power. It is an untapped resource when seeking to identify what works, what is of value. A review of published papers in *Groupwork* did not find any written exclusively by group members, even amongst the articles that explore the outcomes of self-help groups. There were only two where service users appear as co-contributors (Ni Chorcora *et al.*, 1994; Wintram *et al.*, 1994). Articles written by groupworkers do sometimes report the views of group members, but not always in their own words (see, for example, Rhule, 1988). As with other aspects of groupwork, when deciding what and how to evaluate, service users should participate. This helps to ensure ownership of changes (Maggs-Rapport, 2000) – increasing the reality of the group's goals and encouraging commitment to shared objectives. It recognises also that experts by experience and group-workers may diverge in how they conceptualise the issues to be researched (Fisher, 2002).

A second driver is the policy literature – reviews, inspections and inquiries. This driver too is underused, perhaps because standards have yet to be developed in the United Kingdom, unlike in the United States (AASWG, 1999), for groupwork practice. Indeed, the code of conduct (GSCC, 2002) does not directly refer to research and evaluation, nor to what action social (care) workers should take when their employers depart from evidence-based practice. Groupwork's conceptual base is surely sufficiently well-developed to enable standards to be articulated against which practice can be reviewed.

The third driver comprises practitioner perspectives. Practice-generated knowledge is available but, as comments below demonstrate, it is unbalanced for the task of responding to the quality agenda. The same applies to the fourth driver, namely groupwork research in the form of empirical and theoretical accounts, both of practice outcomes and of evaluation methodologies. It also appears to be true that what research-informed knowledge is available is underutilised by groupworkers.

The fifth driver is education for groupwork practice. Again, a subsequent section will explore this driver in more detail. However, this driver is also not delivering its full potential through taught academic and practice curricula. There is also the challenge of triangulating these data sources in order to generate the most power from the conceptual base.

Of the articles published in *Groupwork* between 1988 and 2003 only five focus centrally on evaluation and research. Preston-Shoot (1988) argues that for groupwork to secure a place among methods, evaluation must become an essential feature of practice. His paper outlines the importance of adopting a consciously evaluative approach to groupwork practice and presents a model for evaluating process and outcomes. Peake and Otway (1990) similarly argue that groupwork should be evaluated. For them, one measure of success could be attendance levels, linked to the group's curriculum, rules, selection of members and choice of groupworkers.

Gordon (1992) suggests that, when practice improvement is the aim of evaluation, an illuminative paradigm will provide more valuable information than the traditional experimentalist research paradigm. In the latter a sequence is followed that begins with itemising aims and objectives and continues with generating pre-group measures that can be repeated once groupwork concludes. Conclusions are then drawn from the analysed data. The illuminative paradigm proceeds with a variety of techniques in order to develop an understanding of a group through a process of observation, inquiry, dialogue and explanation.

Harry and colleagues (1997/98) provide an account of a continuous process of evaluation. They advocate a realist approach to evaluation, based on a self-reflexive learning model. A range of methods, sources and times is used, with emphasis on encouraging ownership of evaluation and integrating findings into practice. Finally, Johnson and colleagues (2001) suggest that single-system design is a particularly suitable method of monitoring groupwork practice. They demonstrate how it is possible to use a baseline period as a time for exploration, followed by an intervention period when groupworkers intervene intentionally in group process to effect change. As well as using process records of the group to track movement, they employ pre- and post-group tests to measure change.

A further review of articles published in the first thirteen volumes of *Groupwork* reveals additional interesting findings. For this purpose a threefold division was used, namely:

● Conceptual and theory-building papers, where the contributor's purpose is to develop or review ideas about some aspect of groupwork.
● Descriptive papers, where the contributor's main focus is to describe a group but where some evaluation may be included.
● Empirical papers, where the contributor's focus is to research into groupwork processes and/or outcomes from the perspectives of the different people involved.

Using these criteria for selection, 111 papers were assessed as focusing primarily on research as theory-building and conceptual development. They were designed to develop and/or illustrate part of group work's methodology. In the second category, 104 papers were assessed as principally describing groupwork in practice. Sometimes, usually at a single end point, they contained an evaluation from the groupworkers' and/or members' perspective of what benefits or learning were derived from this experience. Only 17 papers were empirical evaluations (Preston-Shoot, 2004).

Reviewing recent books published in the United Kingdom finds a similar picture. Douglas (2000) does not refer to research or evaluation but in an earlier text (1991) he warns of starting to evaluate practice too late, that is, not at the point of departure. He acknowledges that it can be difficult to assess the quantity and quality of change and to be sure that it is the result of groupwork. He therefore emphasises the importance of well-established baselines and the use of instruments to measure change. Phillips (2001) locates evaluation as part of quality assurance and links it with the setting of clear goals, which provide the framework for subsequent assessment of effectiveness. Observation, feedback sheets and follow-up are amongst the methods recommended.

Barnes and colleagues (1999) devote less than a page to the importance of groupworkers having a research orientation in order to retain curiosity about theory and practice. Doel and Sawdon (1999b) write more expansively about evaluation while denying themselves the space to detail how research methodology might apply to groups. They identify a range of action techniques along-side group discussion, empirical measures and written evaluations. In similar vein, Whitaker (2001) urges groupworkers to monitor and assess groups in order to be self-critical, to inform practice and to articulate beneficial outcomes. She also lists some approaches to evaluation, including post-session reviews and periodic formal reviews. If there are blocks to focusing on evaluation, more could be offered that might enable groupworkers and members alike to explore similar and divergent views about content and process, which would enable them to account to others, to develop the knowledge base, to inform practice and to locate success.

Barriers

Some groupworkers appear quite uncertain about how to review their practice. Clarke and Aimable (1990) did not undertake any formal evaluation of their group with members, recognising that they had underestimated members' ability. They do not appear to have considered what other methods might have been employed to evaluate inputs or outcomes. Tribe and Shackman (1989) recorded that they only felt able to judge the usefulness of the group by the fact that members kept attending and talking of its value. These measures are valuable as sources of evidence but others might have been utilised to explore the sense of community and support that members said they gained. One explanation for the uncertainty might be the limited focus in the groupwork literature on evalua-tion methods. This promotes an assumption that evaluation skills and techniques differ from social work practice generally. It con-tributes to lack of clarity about available methods to disentangle possible variables and illustrate the effect of an intervention.

Another explanation might revolve around training in research and evaluation, both generally and in respect of groupwork. Manor (2003) suggests that groupworkers need to be consciously trained in systematic evaluation. It is arguable that training in research and evaluation methods has been squeezed in the curriculum hitherto in social work education. Similarly squeezed has been groupwork itself, with students reporting that they spend much of their time working with or in groups but feel inadequately prepared for the task (Reid, 1988; Marsh and Triseliotis, 1996; Mathias-Williams and Thomas, 2002). Nor does this appear to be a uniquely United

Kingdom phenomenon (Habermann, 1993; Kurland and Salmon, 1993). Moreover, groupwork and research may be taught as separate rather than overlapping specialisms.

Occupational standards (TOPSS, 2002) and the subject benchmark statement (QAA, 2000) for social work require that practitioners are prepared for and capable of working in and with groups, which includes knowledge and skills for reviewing and evaluating the outcomes of such practice. Both clearly link assessment, planning, goal-setting and evaluation. Professional competence clearly includes the ability to provide evidence for judgements and to monitor effectiveness in meeting need (TOPSS, 2002). It includes using research concepts and tools from social work and other disciplines to understand groups, guide action, support critical reflection and use a range of approaches in evaluating practice outcomes (QAA, 2000). It remains unclear how these educational changes will be reflected in research and evaluation of (learning in) academic and practice curricula and, subsequently, in the groupwork literature.

Perhaps, however, there is also resistance to evaluating practice. O'Connor (1992) has hypothesised that practitioners might have an innate need to demonstrate success. This leads her to argue the need for honesty in evaluation, prioritising critical appraisal through the use of recording and supervision. The theme of defensive evaluation practice appears elsewhere too (Barnes *et al.*, 1999). Having to prove value and effectiveness to those who may be sceptical, rather than seeing evaluation as contributing to a group's development and a practitioner's learning, might lead to a choice of methods most likely to generate good news.

Indeed, it is possible to see the lack of attention to follow-up data in this light. Pennells (1995) noticed that member progress was not sustained after the group concluded. Indeed, it fell to levels below those measured on initial referral. Evaluation may challenge cherished theory. In this instance, the commitment to time-limited groupwork may have resulted in insufficient emphasis being given to consolidation and to working through. Learning and change may decay over time, and it would seem pertinent to explore what factors within groups and post groups enable retention of newly acquired knowledge, skills and attitudes.

Blocks may emanate from perceived difficulties within evaluation. Thus, there is the difficulty of being certain that outcomes are related to the groupwork intervention rather than intervening variables (Johnson *et al.*, 2001). Towl and Dexter (1994) acknowledge the problem of defining and measuring change but move the debate on by identifying a range of tools and by suggesting that data from these be triangulated to overcome the limitations of each technique. The tools include observation, reports, behavioural checklists and questionnaires. Gordon (1992) identifies several reservations about traditional experimentalist research designs. These include ethical issues surrounding use of control groups, oversimplification of goals and insufficient flexibility to incorporate newly emerging needs.

However, groupworkers may be concerned with the very focus on outcomes. Practitioners may fear that the complexity and richness of the groupwork experience will be lost when, in fact, setting goals and monitoring progress improve effectiveness and enhance rather than detract from groupwork. They enable members to experience the satisfaction of achievement. Indeed, the experience of sharing in the measurement of progress towards defined objectives can be therapeutic and motivating.

Sometimes this concern derives from the nature of the group envisaged. Thus, Schneewind (1996) states that a concern with formal evaluation discourages reports of groups that do not have a planned termination date and where membership is self-selected. Maggs-Rapport (2000) writes that it is difficult to conceive outcomes when a project evolves through dialogue with members. Gordon (1992) advocates an illuminative evaluation paradigm for similar reasons, stressing how groups contain multiple realities and how participants influence each other. Rather than outcomes it is evolving processes that should be explored through observation, recording and dialogue. Yet Schneewind (1996) seems concerned with quantitative analysis, perhaps mirroring a more general critique that narrow and positivistic approaches to knowledge and evidence dominate research methods (Humphreys *et al.*, 2003). It should be possible to align evaluative design with a group's structure and to express aims and objectives as outcomes that can then be researched. For example, Otway and Peake (1994) describe a needs-led approach to work with women whose children had been sexually abused. This was an open and open-ended group, where members set the agenda and assessed personal change in terms of the behavioural challenges presented by their children and the stress levels that they experienced as parents.

Sometimes the concern is with outcomes per se. Brown (1996) is critical of the obsession with outcomes because it may lead to a neglect of process and indeed assume that outcomes can be defined. The commitment to improved outcomes for services requires agreement on what outcomes are sought and on how effectiveness is to be understood. Yet what is competent and effective practice is a contested concept. Service users and carers value in professional intervention the quality of relationships and interpersonal and practice skills (Barnes, 2002). Managers, however, appear to prioritise procedural and instrumental skills, knowledge of the law and procedures, while practitioners emphasise process and interpersonal skills, and knowledge from empirical research and of methods of intervention (Marsh and Triseliotis, 1996).

Such reservations about outcomes also connect with anxieties more generally about the quality strategy within the modernisation agenda, namely that it evaluates only what is easily measurable. They may connect too with scepticism that political and managerial commitment does not exist to alter policy or practice in line with evaluation findings (Humphreys *et al.*, 2003).

Additionally, social (care) work has not embraced the idea of the practitioner researcher. Practice has not been defined as a research site, although Whitaker and Archer (1994) suggest that research and practice are comparable and have described one approach whereby researchers, practitioners and managers can engage in producing substantive findings that extend knowledge and understanding. The justification for suggesting that groupworkers adopt a more consciously evaluative approach to their practice is that an essential element of a groupworker's activity is the obligation to appraise their effectiveness. It is difficult otherwise to conceive how groupworkers can comment authoritatively about the needs they encounter, about the impact or effectiveness of social policies, and about the empowering aspects of their practice, without an evidenced practice base. Nor will they be able to challenge how others might construct evidence or seek to marginalise service user and carer narratives. Thus, the justification is to bring a different and empirically supported perspective to needs and problem analysis, to theory and to practice (Kolbo *et al.*, 1997/98; Whitaker, 2001).

The literature conveys an impression of difficulty in connecting with what evaluation methodology may have to offer. Pennells

(1995), in the context of work with bereaved children, writes of the struggle to evaluate effectively and yet uses meetings with families and referrers, questionnaires for children, and group member self-evaluation. Perhaps the problem is not knowing what tools are available and the challenge is demystifying what can count as effective evidence.

A framework for evaluating practice

A systematic review of the research and evaluation literature will provide groupworkers with information about the range of methodologies available. A systematic review of the groupwork literature will provide them with possible outcome criteria (see, for example, Otway and Peake, 1994) and knowledge for practice. Indeed, Pollio (2002) suggests that the evidence-based groupworker should review prior findings when deciding what is current best practice. Accordingly, to search the literature should become one standard for future practice and its dissemination, helping to answer a core social work question – what do I need to know?

Adapting work by Carpenter (2005), it is possible to see how evaluation may focus on:

● Groupworkers' and/or members' reactions – their views of and satisfaction with a group as it evolves over time, and looking back on the experience;
● Modification in attitudes – changes in how they perceive their needs, problems and ways forward, and what facilitated such movement;
● Acquisition of knowledge and skills – changes in how they approach problem-solving and decision-making, and what facilitated such shifts;
● Behavioural change – what groupworkers and/or members actually do differently, and what facilitates and blocks such difference;
● Organisational change – the impact of the group on other stakeholders;
● Benefits to group members, their carers and those they care for – improvements in well-being that may be attributed to the group, including follow-up to assess if and for how long change has endured beyond the group.

It is often unclear from groupwork accounts what persuaded contributors to explore any of the processes and outcomes just outlined. Such analysis could become a second standard for future practice and its dissemination. It revolves around four core social work skills:

1. Survey – what do we need to know?
2. Assessment – where are we now?
3. Goal-setting – where do we need to be?
4. Recording – how will we capture this systematically to demonstrate movement towards goals?

A step-by-step model begins with describing the current situation as precisely as possible, together with desired outcomes (Preston-Shoot, 1988). The intervention is then described, including the methods and resources required, coupled with the indicators to be used to judge progress. Methods and time frames for data-recording and review are then outlined and implemented. Here the focus can be on processes as well as outcomes. Repeat before/during/after group measures can be used rather than the more traditional and limited single point of end of group evaluation.

Manor (2003) describes a process where group members were enabled to identify their goals and then engaged in analysing which learning experiences might promote their realisation. From here it is a small step to delineating the indicators that might suggest movement towards goal achievement (see Preston-Shoot, 1988, for a similar approach). Stating group and individual objectives in terms of processes by which it is hoped the group will be characterised, and outcomes that are expected, is key to aligning evaluation with goals. Connecting evaluation methods with sought goals could become a third standard for future practice and its dissemination.

A fourth standard is triangulation, expanding how evaluation can inform theory and practice by combining methods in order to overcome their individual shortcomings and to avoid the possibility of distortion or bias. Towl and Dexter (1994) make this point when discussing their use of psychometric evaluation of anger management courses. Connecting use of standardised instruments with biographical information, qualitative data and follow-up interviews enables a much richer understanding of what is actually working, for whom, to what degree and for how long.

A fifth standard relates to the number of times information is collected. Despite guidance that identifies evaluation as an aspect of preparation for and beginning to work with groups (Preston-Shoot, 1988), groupworkers appear still to approach it as an ending task, part of the termination phase (Hadlow, 1995; Ross, 1991; Szmagalski, 1989/90). Indeed, such an approach is codified in one set of standards (AASWG, 1999) and may sometimes be related to a lack of resources for integrating assessment and evaluation from the outset (Craig, 1988). This is likely to restrict what can meaningfully be said about group process and outcomes because baseline measures and repeated quantitative and/or qualitative monitoring will not have been used. Much potential material will have been missed or lost. For example, Grindley (1994) used questionnaires to note changes in behaviour and emotions but only as an end rating and self-report. This limits what may be derived as benefits from the group. Lebacq and Shah (1989) recorded and evaluated sessions, including reviews with parents and children, but no baseline measures were taken, again limiting what change may be attributed to the group experience. Mistry's groupwork account (1989) is similar, making it difficult to establish the degree of change in group members' confidence and skills. In none of these examples were follow-up data obtained so it is impossible to know whether progress was maintained after the groups closed.

Methods

Evidence can transform groupwork theory and practice. In relation to what may be termed inputs, the opportunities provided by working in groups, questionnaires, sentence completion and self-reports may be used to rate and describe what members wanted and gained from the group, or what they liked, disliked, remembered and found useful or unhelpful. They may be used to focus on perceptions of whether the group has dealt with its tasks satisfactorily, partially or not at all. Mullender (1995) and Berger (1997–98) provide examples of post-group interviews and questionnaires. These focus on what members liked and gained, what they had expected and what worked best, coupled with what recommendations for improvement they would make. With this approach Szmagalski (1989/90) triangulates indicators of observed behaviour. Kolbo and colleagues (1997/98) include here feedback from service users and analysis of whether the group was implemented as designed.

Monitoring group process over time can be achieved through reviewing monthly objectives (Muir and Notta, 1993) and through observed behaviour, both inside the group and between members outside it. When using observation, groupworkers should be clear what they are looking for and what is important for the purposes of the group. These observations may be described diagrammatically by using sociograms to illustrate, for example, the development of interaction in the group – who talks to whom and who makes what kind of contributions. Rating scales may also be used by members and leaders to offer perspectives at different time frames on the clarity of group goals, the atmosphere in the group, and levels and types of participation.

Monitoring group content over time can be achieved through the use of open-ended evaluation questions at the end of each session (Read *et al.*, 2000), which enables emerging themes to be expressed by group members and/or facilitators. Doel and Sawdon (1999b) also analyse group themes to explore processes and outcomes, and use diagrams to illuminate patterns.

Checklists, for example of members' types of contributions to each session or use of particular behaviours, can track individual outcomes. Measurement scales provide similar information (for examples, see Otway and Peake, 1994; Mullender, 1995), preferably taken at several points before (to provide a baseline), during and after the group. Weisen (1991) used an anxiety inventory and a coping questionnaire, administered pre- and post-group, to provide evidence for effectiveness and therapeutic value. Personal statements and groupworker reports may also be used (Ni Chorcora *et al.*, 1994; Dixon and Phillips, 1994). Self-report should be triangulated with other data, such as cognition scales (Barnett *et al.*, 1990), social support network questionnaires (Hopmeyer and Werk, 1993), or the perceptions of significant others such as parents and teachers, to give authenticity to gains that groupworkers and members believe have been made. Masson and Erooga (1990) used a self-administered questionnaire, which focuses on group members' self-concept, in an early and then concluding group session. This approach enabled the group to identify where there had or had not been individual change and to hypothesise the reasons for this. This evidence was triangulated with feedback from members about the group experience.

Mullender (1988) used discussion, experiential exercises, games and listening to establish a baseline. She then tracked changes in how young people referred to themselves. Craig (1990) used contracts with members and referring social workers to establish a baseline of issues to be worked on, with movement then assessed through rating exercises and proformas. Harry and colleagues (1997/98) used a range of data collection methods, pre- and post-group, including satisfaction questionnaires, interviews with all stakeholders, offender profiles, attendance records, reconviction rates and attitude change scales.

Group and organisational change outcomes can be traced using short-term and long-term appraisals by members, enabling benefits to be identified against initial objectives (see Taylor et al., 1988, for an example drawn from a team development exercise). Finally, the impact of group experience can be assessed by means of follow-up, with group members and/or referrers reporting back (see Hadlow, 1995).

When focusing on evaluating a group it is easy for groupworkers to overlook their own practice – the effect of the group and groupwork on them, the development of their styles of work, their learning and achievements. Researching their own practice should begin at the outset with completion of a personal audit, which can be discussed in supervision.

---

putting into practice: personal audit

> What skills and knowledge do you bring to your practice?
> What are your strengths in groupwork and social (care) work practice?
> What roles and styles come easily to you?
> What do you find difficult in groups?
> What do you hope to contribute to this group?
> In what areas do you wish to improve or develop your practice?
> What are you hoping to learn from working with others in this group?

Next, groupworkers can define indicators that can be used to answer these initial questions and can decide what methods of collecting information will be used. Feedback from group members, including questionnaires, rating scales and interviews, may be used. Sentence completion, discussion with co-workers and supervisors, self-reports and self-rating scales can provide practitioners with information with which to assess progress towards their original objectives. At the conclusion of the group the personal audit can be completed again in order to highlight learning, practice development, future learning needs and knowledge and skill acquisition.

Conclusion

This chapter has sought to reconfigure evaluation as an omnipresent focus throughout groupwork practice, and to transport it from a preoccupation with a single point description to a systematic application of a range of tools at various intervals, selected to be consistent with the type of group. It is founded on the belief that systematic reviews of the literature and of practice will help to energise groupwork's theoretical base and position as a transformative force. This practice shift will require self-examination, as groupworkers reflect on their attitudes towards research and evaluation, review groupwork's conceptual base against emerging evidence, and consider the standards for effective knowledge-informed practice by which they should be held accountable. It will demand ownership (Henchman and Walton, 1997/98) if it is to impact on future practice. It will also require engagement in policy and practice leadership with managers, policy-makers and experts by experience, debating what counts as evidence, as change, as approved practice and as success. Finally, it will require management commitment if it is to influence policy and practice (Humphreys *et al.*, 2003). In so doing new questions will be generated and new curiosities explored, and the evidence accumulated might act as a powerful counterweight to resource-led managerialism.

10 | Integrating groupwork into practice

Transforming experience through groupwork

Professional journals routinely publish accounts of groupwork practice. For instance, Ward (1995), drawing on experiences of community meetings in a children's home, found that it was possible to sustain discussion as children learned from experience that they were taken seriously and that their concerns were of equal concern to others. He was surprised at the capacity of very troubled individuals to make use of groups. Mullender (1990) and Brown (1990) explore the complex patterns of relatedness – mosaics – in residential and day care. They demonstrate how, through whole community meetings and affinity, issue and organised groups, people can negotiate transitions, improve the quality of care offered and received, and manage conflict, authority, intimacy, stress and change.

Braye and Preston-Shoot (2005) describe the core ingredients that enabled a research group of academics, policy-makers, practitioners and experts by experience to talk openly about their perceptions of social work law in action. Increasingly group members replaced polarised assertion with critical testing and interpretation of experience (see Fatout, 1989), which transformed at least some perspectives held when they entered the group. There was a growing willingness and capacity to use differences *for* learning, which shifted people's thinking. Different forms of knowledge and different knowledge-holders were valued. As group members came to trust each other and the group, a reciprocal dialogue became possible, based on respectful listening and questioning, with members prepared to be influenced by others.

These examples show how groupworkers have translated theory into practice. It is to this process of applying groupwork values, knowledge and skills that the book now turns. How can practitioners and agencies develop and embed groupwork in their lived experience of work?

Thinking groupwork

Groupwork knowledge and skills are central to social work practice, organisational management and change, and professional education. Doel (2006) calls this 'group literacy'. Essentially this means drawing on groupwork theory and practice to make sense of and transform such activities as networking and teamworking. The usefulness of this literacy, for teams for example, can be seen when social workers in training are asked to analyse the jury's behaviour in the film *12 Angry Men*. There is rich learning here in respect of group stages, roles and the impact on members of power, discrimination and stereotypes, and leadership and the impact of context and anxiety on the task.

However, groupwork knowledge and skills will have little beneficial impact on research, organisational leadership, staff development and involvement with experts by experience, unless they become integral to each practitioner's mindset and approach to their work. The relevance of this statement is reinforced when considered alongside Heap's comment (1992) that groupworkers have been fumbling, unsystematic and ineffective when trying to engage in organisational change. The challenge arises, therefore, to understand how best to enable practitioners to express and utilise groupwork values, knowledge and skills when engaged in their work, and how to embed groupwork practice in that work.

Training and supervision are important keys here. Evidence indicates that training across groups of staff occupying different job roles, using partnerships or pairs of workers from similar locations, may help to establish groupwork in an agency (Doel and Sawdon, 1999a). However, to impact positively on workers' practice in the longer term, that training will have to enable participants to acquire and integrate knowledge and skills which are seen as facilitating behavioural and practice change. It should enable participants to envisage also how organisational practice might be changed and to capture the benefits for experts by experience from this (new or different) approach to the work (see Carpenter, 2005). Supervision, when not simply preoccupied with standards and quality control, helps to keep that learning alive, to support it through critical incidents, and to apply it to specific groupwork practice and to groupings of which practitioners are a part. It may be formative, with an emphasis on the development of understanding and skills. It may be restorative, enabling groupworkers to feel understood, valued and 'held'. Read and Clements (1999) offer an interesting model that connects training with supervision and organisational change. Managers and practitioners together review performance and the impact of training on practice, and address questions and issues that have arisen with trainers in subsequent follow-up. The objective is to embed training more effectively in individual and agency work, and to impact on policy and practice development.

However, the wider context is another essential key for, without its support for groupwork practice and thinking, learning and motivation may decay and confidence may erode. That context in part is the level of support emanating from the practitioner's agency. Ideally that endorsement will be reflected in a strategy that seeks both to embed groupwork practice in service provision *and* to interrogate all aspects of organisational practice through thinking groups. The former involves tackling the barriers to groupwork practice, such as workloads, the absence of supervision and levels of confidence derived from training. The latter includes drawing on groupwork theory, experience and feedback from groups explicitly for teamwork, inter-agency encounters and project work.

However, in part support for groupwork comes too from mandates, professional, legal, and service user and carer, which provide spaces within which practice can strive to transform people's lived experience. What is apparent is that what is outside any group, and how it is or is not brought into a group or grouping, will influence the ability of practitioners and experts by experience to utilise groupwork knowledge and skills effectively, and to promote groups as creative ways of working.

The social work education (for instance, Burgess and Taylor, 1995), teamwork (Vernelle, 1994) and research literature (for example, Braye and Preston-Shoot, 2005), reveals several other keys for establishing groups in particular and utilising groupwork knowledge and skills more generally within practice and the management of practice. These keys are focus, process, facilitation, task, structure and members.

In any group or team there are four areas on which to focus – first the group as a whole, second the individuals within it, next the environment or context for the group, and finally its individual members. It may prove helpful to keep under review a force field analysis of these four areas, namely what facilitates and what blocks individuals and the group from making desired contributions, since this will help those responsible for providing leadership to determine how to intervene.

One key aspect of process is recognising and using the awareness of stages in group or team development to guide action. Another is recognising how individuals are growing into and taking up roles within the group. Once again, a force field analysis may help to identify blocks and ways to respond. Recognition of stages may inform leadership decisions, for instance on how to open meetings, to set the tone for the work, or to respond to the expression of emotions and difference. At some points, especially early on in any grouping, it may be necessary to contain and hold emotional responses to the work and lack of consensus. Later on in a group's existence, it may be possible to explore what may be learned from difference and diversity and, indeed, to draw on the resources available to highlight experience and perspective as a way of opening up dialogue and debate.

Process leadership also involves considering the availability of resources and whether these are sufficient for the task. Thus, what skills and knowledge for different roles do members bring, and does the context support and enable this use of diversity? Throughout the question of power must be acknowledged. In social work education, this will revolve around assessment. In research it will turn on control of the boundaries of the agenda and task, while in organisations it may concern who can exercise leadership. In all settings it is a question of ensuring that all voices are privileged, that is, located to participate in knowledge development.

Of the many responsibilities on facilitators or leaders, a number emerge as particularly significant. They should be open to challenge and to learning if members are not to become cynical about the degree of involvement or power being offered. They have to balance when to steer or guide and when to encourage self-direction, for which an analysis of individual and group stages of development may prove helpful. Skill in offering and in encouraging the giving of feedback is one aspect of a more general orientation. This aims to bring out individual and group strengths and skills, to pinpoint and release how these resources might contribute to the task, and to demonstrate how changes in their expression might take the work further forward.

In each setting the task must be focused and structured, with those involved accepting that its achievement is inextricably bound up with group process. The structure should be one that facilitates rather than blocks communication. Aims should be realistic when considered against the resources available. Time, pace and venue all influence how individuals and the group engage with the task. A structure that encourages a culture of creativity and exploration is much more likely to foster learning than one in which people are defensive about their own positions.

Finally, the practice that informs this discussion emphasises the members themselves. They should feel valued and involved as far as possible from the outset. A key here is the provision of information and clarity about the degree of control they can exercise over the construction of the task. The more communication is open, conflict worked through rather than repressed, and aims and methods negotiated, the more members may feel encouraged to commit themselves and to consider that the benefits of involvement outweigh the risks or costs. In any event, involvement should leave members feeling and believing that they are stronger than before their involvement, for instance in terms of the learning derived from and the personal resources acquired through the experience.

In many respects what has just been described as axiomatic of groupwork is the essence of social work more generally. Perhaps when groupworkers are envisaging what it means to 'think groups', they might feel encouraged if they search for the similarities with rather than the differences between groupwork and social work values, knowledge and skills. Put another way, it might be helpful to envisage those practice situations in which practitioners draw upon groupwork knowledge, values and skills.

Assessment, intervention and review, increasingly multi-professional and inter-agency, require clarity of communication and purpose, a sharing and integration of perspectives, and agreement about roles and norms. Social (care) work involves the management of interdependence and multiple relationships. Here it will be essential to tune into the emotional climate as well as to monitor oneself and others if engagement in the work is to be effective. There will be set events, critical incidents that often revolve around dilemmas and strongly held emotions and perceptions, and less formalised spaces where opportunities may arise for purposeful work. Effectiveness here may depend, at least in part, on the clarity of goals and tasks, and acceptance of these by those present. Crucial too will be the adequacy of resources, which includes time and the attributes or skills for different aspects of task and/or process brought to the interaction by those taking part. Amongst these skills are initiating or evaluating work, keeping track of progress, monitoring emotional climate and involvement, or moving on through questioning or providing information. Effectiveness may depend also on the willingness of members, whether or not they hold formal leadership roles, to accept responsibility for building cohesion, for tackling problems that affect connection, for providing structure and for promoting interaction. The impact of power, in terms of how it is used or perceived, may result in compliant decision-making, where questioning and difference are discouraged. Alternatively, such groupings, teams or networks may be characterised by an opportunity to explore perceptions, to use and reflect on feedback, to learn from group process about the work being undertaken and to address divergence or conflict openly.

The increasing use of advocacy in social (care) services for young people and for adults requiring care or services opens up the possibility of collective action. The lived experience of work for staff and volunteers can be managed more effectively when their vulnerability to anxiety and stress is reduced by facilitating their membership of a collective that can focus on the issues and problems they encounter and the context of which they are a part. Bringing people together can reduce isolation, promote belonging, enhance awareness and broaden perspectives as a prelude to promoting understanding and influencing policy and practice. As with other networks, team or groupings, this process can lead to systems and relationship change through the creation of a learning environment. Moreover, in a policy context frequently dominated by the requirement to deliver outcomes, thinking groups involves seeing, naming and using process to facilitate effective working together. Groupwork informs this work. However, groupwork skills, knowledge and values can also be informed by it.

Nonetheless, irrespective of the degree of preparation as a result of academic and practice learning, of which reading this book might be one element, it may still appear daunting to 'think groups' or to draw on groupwork knowledge and skills in encounters with teams and groupings. An understandable personal need for success might be a constraining force, which the availability of supervision might contain. Prior education and training experiences, where groupwork has been the subject and/or the medium for learning, might act as either facilitating or constraining forces. Emerging partnerships with other professionals, consequent upon organisational change in health and social care, and with experts by experience due to changes in the governance of social work education and practice, might stimulate working with groups to research gaps in service and deliver new provision. To the degree that thinking and working in/with groups does appear daunting, an individual action plan may help.

---

putting into practice: taking stock

➤ What have you learned recently about groups and groupwork? How has your mindset about groups and groupings shifted as a result of this learning?
➤ In what ways could you integrate this learning in your interaction with groupings and/or your groupwork practice?
➤ How would you currently evaluate strengths and weaknesses in your skills in groupwork and interaction with groupings?
➤ What action might you take to maximise the strengths and to address these weaknesses?
➤ Over what time span and with whose help will you take this action?

Research knowledge, professional practice wisdom, and service user and carer perspectives about groups and groupings, not forgetting one's own experience, will not remain static. An individual action plan, regularly updated, is one strategy for seeking to capture and draw on that learning for continuing professional development which, indeed, was one of the hallmarks of a professional long before the social policy modernisation agenda emphasised its importance to quality and accountable standards.

Groupwork, as with social work more generally, is not just a technical activity, competence for which can be achieved by learning methods. Clearly, competence in applying technical knowledge is important and this book is one attempt to provide such a solid foundation. However, groupwork and social work also engage with profound and complex social issues. People with severe mental distress and people who are seeking asylum are members of groups frequently dehumanised in policy pronouncements. The narratives of experts by experience are sometimes valued and sometimes dismissed by policy-makers. The rights of different groups, for example fathers separated from their children as a result of relationship breakdown, have to be balanced in policy terms and in the unique circumstances of individual cases. Social (care) workers, whether or not groupworkers, have to engage with these and other social questions. This requires a practice that recognises and engages with human rights and social justice, for instance through partnership working, advocacy and consultation. It also requires ethical or moral practice, capable of articulating and working through different options, balancing competing imperatives and negotiating practice dilemmas. While groupwork may appear challenging, it is also very necessary as part of social (care) work's engagement with social issues and the people most immediately affected by them.

Bibliography

AASWG (1999) *Standards for Social Work Practice with Groups.* Akron, OH: Association for the Advancement of Social Work with Groups.

Adams, R. (1990) *Self-Help, Social Work and Empowerment.* London: Macmillan.

Arnstein, S. (1969) 'A ladder of citizen participation', *Journal of the American Institute of Planners*, 35, July, 215–24.

Audit Commission (2002) *Recruitment and Retention: A Public Service Workforce for the 21st Century.* London: The Stationery Office.

Barnes, B., Ernst, S. and Hyde, K. (1999) *An Introduction to Groupwork: A Group-Analytic Perspective.* London: Macmillan.

Barnes, J. (2002) *Focus on the Future: Key Messages from Focus Groups about the Future of Social Work Training.* London: Department of Health.

Barnett, S., Corder, F. and Jehu, D. (1990) 'Group treatment for women sex offenders against children', *Groupwork*, 3(2), 191–203.

Behroozi, C. (1992) 'Groupwork with involuntary clients: remotivating strategies', *Groupwork*, 5(2), 31–41.

Bensted, J., Brown, A., Forbes, C. and Wall, R. (1994) 'Men working with men in groups: masculinity and crime', *Groupwork*, 7(1), 37–49.

Berger, R. (1997–98) 'Suddenly the light went on: using groupwork to empower returning students', *Groupwork*, 10(1), 21–9.

Bion, W. (1961) *Experiences in Groups.* London: Tavistock.

Blacklock, N. (2003) 'Gender awareness and the role of the groupworker in programmes for domestic violence perpetrators', in M. Cohen and A. Mullender (eds) *Gender and Groupwork.* London: Routledge.

Bodinham, H. and Weinstein, J. (1991) 'Making authority accountable: the experience of a statutory based women's group', *Groupwork*, 4(1), 22–30.

Bradshaw, J. (1972) 'The concept of social need', *New Society*, 19 (496), 640–3.

Braye, S. and Preston-Shoot, M. (1995) *Empowering Practice in Social Care.* Buckingham: Open University Press.

Braye, S. and Preston-Shoot, M. (2005) 'Emerging from out of the shadows? Service user and carer involvement in systematic reviews', *Evidence and Policy*, 1(2), 173–93.

Braye, S. and Preston-Shoot, M., with Cull, L.-A., Johns, R. and Roche, J. (2005) *Teaching, Learning and Assessment of Law in Social Work Education*. London: Social Care Institute for Excellence.

Breton, M. (1991) 'Toward a model of social groupwork practice with marginalised populations', *Groupwork*, 4(1), 31–47.

Brown, A. (1990) 'Groupwork with a difference: the group "mosaic" in residential and day care settings', *Groupwork*, 3(3), 269–85.

Brown, A. (1996) 'Groupwork into the future: some personal reflections', *Groupwork*, 9(1), 80–96.

Brown, A. (1997) 'Groupwork', in M. Davies (ed.) *The Blackwell Companion to Social Work*. Oxford: Blackwell.

Brown, A., Caddick, B., Gardiner, M. and Sleeman, S. (1982) 'Towards a British model of groupwork', *British Journal of Social Work*, 12(6), 587–603.

Burgess, H. and Taylor, I. (1995) 'Facilitating enquiry and action learning groups for social work education', *Groupwork*, 8(2), 117–33.

Caddick, B. (1991) 'Using groups in working with offenders: a survey of groupwork in the probation services of England and Wales', *Groupwork*, 4(3), 197–214.

Carpenter, J. (2005) *Evaluating Outcomes in Social Work Education*. London and Dundee: Social Care Institute for Excellence and Scottish Institute for Excellence in Social Work Education.

Clarke, J., Cochrane, A. and McLaughlin, E. (eds) (1994) *Managing Social Policy*. London: Sage.

Clarke, P. and Aimable, A. (1990) 'Groupwork techniques in a residential primary school for emotionally disturbed boys', *Groupwork*, 3(1), 36–48.

Cohen, M. (2003) 'Women in groups: the history of feminist empowerment', in M. Cohen and A. Mullender (eds) *Gender and Groupwork*. London: Routledge.

Cohen, M. and Mullender, A. (eds) (2003) *Gender and Groupwork*. London: Routledge.

Cowburn, M. (1990) 'Work with male sex offenders in groups', *Groupwork*, 3(2), 157–71.

Craig, E. (1990) 'Starting the journey: enhancing the therapeutic elements of groupwork with adolescent female child sexual abuse victims', *Groupwork*, 3(2), 103–17.

Craig, R. (1988) 'Structured activities with adolescent boys', *Groupwork*, 1(1), 48–59.

Davies, M. (1984) 'Training: what we think of it now', *Social Work Today*, 15(20), 12–17.

DeLois, K. (2003) 'Genderbending: reflections on group work with queer youth', in M. Cohen and A. Mullender (eds) Gender and Groupwork. London: Routledge.

DH (1998) Modernising Social Services. London: The Stationery Office.

DH (1999) Working Together to Safeguard Children: A Guide to Inter-Agency Working to Safeguard and Promote the Welfare of Children. London: The Stationery Office.

DH (2000a) The Quality Protects Programme: Transforming Children's Services 2001–2002 (LAC (2000)22). London: Department of Health.

DH (2000b) Guidance on Good Practice in Compiling and Maintaining Records (LASSL (2000)2). London: Department of Health.

DH (2002) Requirements for Social Work Training. London: Department of Health.

Dixon, G. and Phillips, M. (1994) 'A psychotherapeutic group for boys who have been sexually abused', Groupwork, 7(1), 79–95.

Doel, M. (2006) Using Groupwork. London: Routledge.

Doel, M. and Sawdon, C. (1999a) 'No group is an island: groupwork in a social work agency', Groupwork, 11(3), 50–69.

Doel, M. and Sawdon, C. (1999b) The Essential Groupworker: Teaching and Learning Creative Groupwork. London: Jessica Kingsley.

Doel, M. and Sawdon, C. (2001) 'What makes for successful groupwork? A survey of agencies in the UK', British Journal of Social Work, 31, 435–51.

Donnellan, P. (1981) 'Supervision in groupwork', in S. Martel (ed.) Supervision and Team Support. London: Bedford Square Press.

Douglas, T. (1991) A Handbook of Common Groupwork Problems. London: Routledge.

Douglas, T. (2000) Basic Groupwork, 2nd edn. London: Routledge.

Dowling, E. (1979) 'Co-therapy: a clinical researcher's view', in S. Walrond-Skinner (ed.) Family and Marital Psychotherapy. London: Routledge & Kegan Paul.

Everitt, A., Hardiker, P., Littlewood, J. and Mullender, A. (1992) Applied Research for Better Practice. London: Macmillan.

Fatout, M. (1989) 'Decision-making in therapeutic groups', Groupwork, 2(1), 70–9.

Fatout, M. (1997/98) 'Exploring worker responses to critical incidents', Groupwork, 10(3), 183–95.

Fisher, M. (2002) 'The role of service users in problem formulation and technical aspects of social research', Social Work Education, 21(3), 305–12.

Fitzsimmons, J. and Levy, R. (1996) 'An art therapy group for young people with eating difficulties', Groupwork, 9(3), 283–91.

Garrett, P. (1995) 'Group dialogue within prisons', Groupwork, 8(1), 49–66.

Gobat, H. (1993) 'Groupwork with parents of learning disabled adolescents', *Groupwork*, 6(3), 221–31.

Godfrey, M. and Callaghan, G. (2000) *Exploring Unmet Need: The Challenge of a User-Centred Response*. York: Joseph Rowntree Foundation.

Gordon, K. (1992) 'Evaluation for the improvement of groupwork practice', *Groupwork*, 5(1), 34–49.

Green, R. (2000) 'Applying a community needs profiling approach to tackling service user poverty', *British Journal of Social Work*, 30(3), 287–303.

Grindley, G. (1994) 'Working with religious communities', *Groupwork*, 7(1), 50–62.

Groves, P. and Schondel, C. (1997/98) 'Feminist groupwork with lesbian survivors of incest', *Groupwork*, 10(3), 215–30.

GSCC (2002) *Codes of Practice for Social Care Workers and Employers*. London: General Social Care Council.

Gutierrez, L. (1990) 'Working with women of color: an empowerment perspective', *Social Work*, 35(2), 149–53.

Habermann, U. (1990) 'Self-help groups: a minefield for professionals', *Groupwork*, 3(3), 221–35.

Habermann, U. (1993) 'Why groupwork is not put into practice: reflections on the social work scene in Denmark', *Groupwork*, 6(1), 17–29.

Hadlow, J. (1995) 'Groupwork to facilitate family reconstitution: a social work response', *Groupwork*, 8(3), 313–23.

Hare, P., Baxter, M. and Newbronner, E. (2002) 'Taking a count of vulnerable children', *Community Care*, 24–30 January, 40–1.

Harry, R., Hegarty, P., Lisles, C., Thurston, R. and Vanstone, M. (1997–98) 'Research into practice does go: integrating research within programme development', *Groupwork*, 10(2), 107–25.

Hartford, M. (1972) *Groups in Social Work*. New York: Columbia University Press.

Hayden, A., Hopkinson, J., Sengendo, J. and von Rabenau, E. (1999) 'It ain't (just) what you do, it's the way that you do it: working towards effective practice in probation groupwork', *Groupwork*, 11(1), 41–53.

Heap, K. (1966) 'The groupworker as central person', *Case Conference*, 12(7), 20–9.

Heap, K. (1992) 'The European groupwork scene: where were we? Where are we? Where are we going?' *Groupwork*, 5(1), 9–23.

Henchman, D. and Walton, S. (1997–98) 'Effective groupwork packages and the importance of process', *Groupwork*, 10(1), 70–80.

Henry, M. (1988) 'Revisiting open groups', *Groupwork*, 1(3), 215–28.

Hill, A. (2001) ' "No-one else could understand": women's experiences of a support group run by and for mothers of sexually abused children', *British Journal of Social Work*, 31(3), 385–97.

Hodge, J. (1985) *Planning for Co-leadership: A Practice Guide for Groupworkers*. Newcastle: Groupvine.

Home, A. (1996) 'Enhancing research usefulness with adapted focus groups', *Groupwork*, 9(2), 128–38.

Hopmeyer, E. and Werk, A. (1993) 'A comparative study of four family bereavement groups', *Groupwork*, 6(2), 107–21.

Humphreys, C., Berridge, D., Butler, I. and Ruddick, R. (2003) 'Making research count: the development of knowledge-based practice', *Research Policy and Planning*, 21(1), 11–9.

Hunt, G. (ed.) (1998) *Whistleblowing in the Social Services*. London: Arnold.

IASSW (2001) *International Definition of Social Work*. Copenhagen: International Association of Schools of Social Work and the International Federation of Social Workers.

James, A. (1994) *Managing to Care*. London: Longman.

Janis, I. (1972) *Victims of Groupthink: A Psychological Study of Foreign Policy Decisions and Fiascos*. Boston, MA: Houghton Mifflin.

Johnson, P., Beckerman, A. and Auerbach, C. (2001) 'Researching our own practice: single system design for groupwork', *Groupwork*, 13(1), 57–72.

Jones, C. (2001) 'Voices from the front line: state social workers and New Labour', *British Journal of Social Work*, 31(4), 547–62.

Kohli, K. (1993) 'Groupwork with deaf people', *Groupwork*, 6(3), 232–47.

Kolbo, J., Horn, K. and Randall, E. (1997/98) 'Implementing a novel groupwork model: application of an innovation–developmental process', *Groupwork*, 10(1), 41–54.

Kurland, R. and Salmon, R. (1993) 'Groupwork versus casework in a group', *Groupwork*, 6(1), 5–16.

Laming, H. (2003) *Inquiry into the Death of Victoria Climbié*. London: The Stationery Office.

LASSL (2000) *New Guidance on Planning Children's Services*. London: Department of Health.

Lebacq, M. and Shah, Z. (1989) 'A group for black and white sexually abused children', *Groupwork*, 2(2), 123–33.

Lee, J. (1991) 'Empowerment through mutual aid groups: a practice grounded conceptual framework', *Groupwork*, 4(1), 5–21.

Lee, J. (1999) 'Crossing bridges: groupwork in Guyana', *Groupwork*, 11(1), 6–23.

Lizzio, A. and Wilson, K. (2001) 'Facilitating group beginnings 1: a practice model', *Groupwork*, 13(1), 6–30.

Loosley, S. and Mullender, A. (2003) 'Gendering work with children and youth: groups for child witnesses of woman abuse', in M. Cohen and A. Mullender (eds) *Gender and Groupwork*. London: Routledge.

Lordan, N. (1996) 'The use of sculpt in social groupwork education', *Groupwork*, 9(1), 62–79.

Lumley, J. and Marchant, H. (1989) 'Learning about groupwork', *Groupwork*, 2(2), 134–44.

Lymbery, M. (2001) 'Social work at the crossroads', *British Journal of Social Work*, 31(3), 369–84.

Maggs-Rapport, F. (2000) 'Teenagers' experiences of a health promotion project', *Groupwork*, 12(3), 5–20.

Malekoff, A. (1999) 'Expressing our anger: hindrance or help in groupwork with adolescents', *Groupwork*, 11(1), 71–82.

Manor, O. (1988) 'Preparing the client for social groupwork: an illustrated framework', *Groupwork*, 1(2), 100–14.

Manor, O. (1989) 'Organising accountability for social groupwork: more choices', *Groupwork*, 2(2), 108–22.

Manor, O. (2003) 'Groupwork fit for purpose? An inclusive framework for mental health', *Groupwork*, 13(3), 101–28.

Marchant, H. (1988) 'Integrating groupwork methods and practice in the curriculum', in A. Brown, J. Lumley, H. Marchant, R. Morgan-Jones and P. Smith (eds) *Training Social Workers for Group Work*. London: NISW.

Marsh, P. and Triseliotis, J. (1996) *Ready to Practise? Social Workers and Probation Officers: Their Training and First Year in Work*. Aldershot: Avebury.

Masson, H. and Erooga, M. (1990) 'The forgotten parent: groupwork with mothers of sexually abused children', *Groupwork*, 3(2), 144–56.

Mathias-Williams, R. and Thomas, N. (2002) 'Great expectations? The career aspirations of social work students', *Social Work Education*, 21(4), 421–35.

Matzat, J. (1993) 'Away with experts? Self-help groupwork in Germany', *Groupwork*, 6(1), 30–42.

Mayer, J. and Timms, N. (1970) *The Client Speaks*. London: Routledge & Kegan Paul.

McKernan McKay, M., Garcia, T., Scally, J. and Martinez, L. (1996) 'A collaborative group approach for urban parents', *Groupwork*, 9(1), 15–26.

McLeod, E. (2003) 'Grouping together for equality in physical health', in M. Cohen and A. Mullender (eds) *Gender and Groupwork*. London: Routledge.

Mistry, T. (1989) 'Establishing a feminist model of groupwork in the probation service', *Groupwork*, 2(2), 145–58.

Mistry, T. and Brown, A. (1991) 'Black/white co-working in groups', *Groupwork*, 4(2), 101–18.

Muir, L. and Notta, H. (1993) 'An Asian mother's group', *Groupwork*, 6(2), 122–32.

Mullender, A. (1988) 'Groupwork as the method of choice with black children in white foster homes', *Groupwork*, 1(2), 158–72.

Mullender, A. (1990) 'Groupwork in residential settings for elderly people', *Groupwork*, 3(3), 286–301.

Mullender, A. (1991) 'Nottingham advocacy group: giving a voice to the users of mental health services', *Practice*, 5(1), 5–12.

Mullender, A. (1995) 'Groups for children who have lived with domestic violence: learning from North America', *Groupwork*, 8(1), 79–98.

Mullender, A. (1996) 'Groupwork with male "domestic" abusers: models and dilemmas', *Groupwork*, 9(1), 27–47.

Mullender, A. and Ward, D. (1985) 'Towards an alternative model of social groupwork', *British Journal of Social Work*, 15(2), 155–72.

Mullender, A. and Ward, D. (1989) 'Challenging familiar assumptions: preparing for and initiating a self-directed group', *Groupwork*, 2(1), 5–26.

Mullender, A. and Ward, D. (1991) *Self-Directed Groupwork: Users Take Action for Empowerment*. London: Whiting & Birch.

Mulvie, C. (1991) Groupwork in the Luton probation and bail hostel', *Groupwork*, 4(3), 249–61.

Ni Chorcora, M., Jennings, E. and Lordan, N. (1994) 'Issues of empowerment: anti-oppressive groupwork by disabled people in Ireland', *Groupwork*, 7(1), 63–78.

Nosko, A. and Breton, M. (1997/98) 'Applying a strengths, competence and empowerment model', *Groupwork*, 10(1), 55–69.

O'Connor, I. (1992) 'Bereaved by suicide: setting up an "ideal" therapy group in a real world', *Groupwork*, 5(3), 74–86.

Otway, O. and Peake, A. (1994) 'Using a facilitated self help group for women whose children have been sexually abused', *Groupwork*, 7(2), 153–62.

Papell, C. (1992) 'Groupwork from across the Atlantic: its identity and diffusion', *Groupwork*, 5(1), 5–8.

Papell, C. (1999) 'Technical errors or missed alternatives: an interview with Catherine Papell', *Groupwork*, 11(1), 83–93.

Papell, C. and Rothman, B. (1966) 'Social group work models: possession and heritage', *Journal of Education for Social Work*, 2(2), 66–77.

Pawson, R., Boaz, A., Grayson, L., Long, A. and Barnes, C. (2003) *Types and Quality of Knowledge in Social Care*. London: Social Care Institute for Excellence.

Payne, M. (1997) *Modern Social Work Theory*. London: Macmillan.

Peake, A. and Otway, O. (1990) 'Evaluating success in groupwork: why not measure the obvious?', *Groupwork*, 3(2), 118–33.

Pease, B. (2003) 'Critical reflections on profeminist practice in men's groups', in M. Cohen and A. Mullender (eds) *Gender and Groupwork*. London: Routledge.

Pennells, M. (1995) 'Time and space to grieve: a bereavement group for children', *Groupwork*, 8(3), 243–54.

Percy-Smith, J. (1992) 'Auditing social needs', *Policy and Politics*, 20(1), 29–34.

Percy-Smith, J. (ed.) (1996) *Needs Assessments in Public Policy*. Buckingham: Open University Press.

Phillips, J. (2001) *Groupwork in Social Care*. London: Jessica Kingsley.

Pollio, D. (2002) 'The evidence-based group worker', *Social Work with Groups*, 25(4), 57–70.

Preston-Shoot, M. (1986) 'Co-leadership in groups: decision or drift?', in P. Wedge and C. Pritchard (eds) *Proceedings of the First Annual Conference, Research Related to Practice*. Birmingham: JUC/BASW.

Preston-Shoot, M. (1988) 'A model for evaluating groupwork', *Groupwork*, 1(2), 147–57.

Preston-Shoot, M. (1989) 'Using contracts in groupwork', *Groupwork*, 2(1), 36–47.

Preston-Shoot, M. (1992) 'On empowerment, partnership and authority in groupwork practice: a training contribution', *Groupwork*, 5(2), 5–30.

Preston-Shoot, M. (1995) 'Assessing anti-oppressive practice', Social Work Education, 14(2), 11–29.

Preston-Shoot, M. (2000) 'What if? Using the law to uphold practice values and standards', *Practice*, 12(4), 49–63.

Preston-Shoot, M. (2001) 'Regulating the road of good intentions: observations on the relationship between policy, regulations and practice in social work', *Practice*, 13(4), 5–20.

Preston-Shoot, M. (2003a) 'Changing learning and learning change: making a difference in education, policy and practice', *Journal of Social Work Practice*, 17(1), 9–23.

Preston-Shoot, M. (2003b) 'A matter of record', *Practice*, 15(3), 31–50.

Preston-Shoot, M. (2003c) 'Only connect: client, carer and professional perspectives on community care assessment processes', *Research Policy and Planning*, 21(3), 23–35.

Preston-Shoot, M. (2004) 'Evidence: the final frontier? Star Trek, groupwork and the mission of change', *Groupwork*, 14(3), 18–43.

Preston-Shoot, M. and Agass, D. (1990) *Making Sense of Social Work: Psychodynamics, Systems and Practice*. London: Macmillan.

Pugh, G. and De'Ath, E. (1989) *Working Towards Partnership in the Early Years*. London: National Children's Bureau.

QAA (2000) *Subject Benchmark Statements: Social Policy and Administration and Social Work*. Gloucester: Quality Assurance Agency for Higher Education.

Raynes, N., Temple, B., Glenister, C. and Coulthard, L. (2001) *Quality at Home for Older People: Involving Service Users in Defining Home Care Specifications*. Bristol: Policy Press.

Read, J. and Clements, L. (1999) 'Research, the law and good practice in relation to disabled children: an approach to staff development in a local authority', *Local Governance*, 25(2), 87–95.

Read, S., Papakosta-Harvey, V. and Bower, S. (2000) 'Using workshops on loss for adults with learning disabilities', *Groupwork*, 12(2), 6–26.

Reder, P. and Duncan, S. (1999) *Lost Innocents: A Follow-up Study of Fatal Child Abuse*. London: Routledge.

Reder, P., Duncan, S. and Gray, M. (1993) *Beyond Blame: Child Abuse Tragedies Revisited*. London: Routledge.

Reid, K. (1988) ' "But I don't want to lead a group!" Some common problems of social workers leading groups', *Groupwork*, 1(2), 6–26.

Reynolds, J. and Shackman, J. (1994) 'Partnership in training and practice with refugees', *Groupwork*, 7(1), 23–36.

Rhule, C. (1988) 'A group for white women with black children', *Groupwork*, 1(1), 41–7.

Rice, S. and Goodman, C. (1992) 'Support groups for older people: is homogeneity or heterogeneity the answer?', *Groupwork*, 5(2), 65–77.

Ross, S. (1991) 'The termination phase in groupwork: tasks for the groupworker', *Groupwork*, 4(10), 57–70.

Schiller, L. (2003) 'Women's group development from a relational model and a new look at facilitator influence on group development', in M. Cohen and A. Mullender (eds) *Gender and Groupwork*. London: Routledge.

Schneewind, F. (1996) 'Support groups for families of confused elders: issues surrounding open peer-led groups', *Groupwork*, 9(3), 303–19.

Senior, P. (1991) 'Groupwork in the probation service: care or control in the 1990s', *Groupwork*, 4(3), 284–95.

Sheppard, D. (1996) *Learning the Lessons*, 2nd edn. London: The Zito Trust.

Shulman, L. (1988) 'Groupwork practice with hard to reach clients: a modality of choice', *Groupwork*, 1(1), 5–16.

Smith, P. (1988) 'In search of the well-rounded groupworker: teaching for a choice of appropriate intervention skills', in A. Brown, J. Lumley, H. Marchant, R. Morgan-Jones and P. Smith (eds) *Training Social Workers for Group Work*. London: NISW.

Springer, D., Pomeroy, E. and Johnson, T. (1999) 'A group intervention for children of incarcerated parents: initial blunders and subsequent solutions', *Groupwork*, 11(1), 54–70.

SSI (1999) *Planning to Deliver*. London: Department of Health.

Stratton, P., Preston-Shoot, M. and Hanks, H. (1990) *Family Therapy Training and Practice*. Birmingham: Venture Press.

Sunderland, C. (1997/98) 'Brief group therapy and the use of metaphor', *Groupwork*, 10(2), 126–41.

Swift, P. (1996) 'Focusing on groups in social policy research', *Groupwork*, 9(2), 154–68.

Szmagalski, J. (1989/90) 'Staff development through groupwork in Polish community agencies: the 'centres of culture''', *Groupwork*, 2(3), 237–47.

Taylor, J., Miles, D. and Eastgate, J. (1988) 'A team development exercise', *Groupwork*, 1(3), 252–61.

Thiara, R. (2003) 'Difference, collective action and women's groups: South Asian women in Britain', in M. Cohen and A. Mullender (eds) *Gender and Groupwork*. London: Routledge.

TOPSS (2002) *The National Occupational Standards for Social Work*. Leeds: Training Organisation for the Personal Social Services.

Towl, G. and Dexter, P. (1994) 'Anger management groupwork with prisoners: an empirical evaluation', *Groupwork*, 7(3), 256–69.

Tribe, R. (1997/98) 'A critical analysis of a support and clinical supervision group for interpreters working with refugees located in Britain', *Groupwork*, 10(3), 196–214.

Tribe, R. and Shackman, J. (1989) 'A way forward: a group for refugee women', *Groupwork*, 2(2), 159–66.

Tuckman, B. (1965) 'Developmental sequences in small groups', *Psychological Bulletin*, 63, 384–99.

Turkie, A. (1992) 'Supporting those who support others: the groupwork consultant's role in facilitating work groups', *Groupwork*, 5(1), 24–33.

Vernelle, B. (1994) *Understanding and Using Groups*. London: Whiting & Birch.

Walter, I., Nutley, S., Percy-Smith, J., McNeish, D. and Frost, S. (2004) *Improving the Use of Research in Social Care Practice*. London: Social Care Institute for Excellence.

Walton, P. (1996) 'Focus groups and familiar social work skills: their contribution to practitioner research', *Groupwork*, 9(2), 139–53.

Ward, A. (1993) 'The large group: the heart of the system in group care', *Groupwork*, 6(1), 64–77.

Ward, A. (1995) 'Establishing community meetings in a children's home', *Groupwork*, 8(1), 67–78.

Ward, D. (1996) Editorial, *Groupwork*, 9(2), 107–9.

Ward, D. (2002) 'Groupwork', in R. Adams, L. Dominelli and M. Payne (eds) *Social Work: Themes, Issues and Critical Debates*, 2nd edn. Basingstoke: Palgrave Macmillan.

Ward, D. and Mullender, A. (1991) 'Facilitation in self-directed groupwork', *Groupwork*, 4(2), 141–51.

Waterhouse, R. (2000) *Lost in Care: The Report of the Tribunal of Inquiry into the Abuse of Children in Care in the Former County*

Council Areas of Gwynedd and Clwyd since 1974. London: The Stationery Office.

Weinstein, J. (1994) 'A dramatic view of groupwork', *Groupwork*, 7(3), 248–55.

Weisen, R. (1991) 'Evaluative study of groupwork for stress and anxiety', *Groupwork*, 4(2), 152–62.

Whitaker, D. (2001) *Using Groups to Help People*, 2nd edn. Hove: Brunner-Routledge.

Whitaker, D. and Archer, L. (1994) 'Partnership research and its contributions to learning and to team-building', *Social Work Education*, 13(3), 39–60.

Williams, M. (1966) 'Limitations, fantasies and security operations of beginning group psychotherapists', *International Journal of Group Psychotherapy*, 16, 150–62.

Williams, O. (2003) 'Developing the capacity to address social context issues: group treatment with African American men who batter', in M. Cohen and A. Mullender (eds) *Gender and Groupwork*. London: Routledge.

Wintram, C., Chamberlain, K., Kuhn, M. and Smith, J. (1994) 'A time for women: an account of a group for women on an out of city housing development in Leicester', *Groupwork*, 7(2), 125–35.

Yalom, I. (1995) *The Theory and Practice of Group Psychotherapy*, 4th edn. New York: Basic Books.

Author index

Subject index